MEMORIES
of
Newburyport, Massachusetts
by
Henry Bailey Little
1851-1957

Compiled by Margaret Peckham Motes

MEMORIES
of
Newburyport, Massachusetts
by
Henry Bailey Little
1851-1957

Copyright © 2019, Margaret Peckham Motes. All rights reserved. No part of this book may be reproduced without the express permission of the author except when quoted and referenced.

ISBN: 978-0-80635-949-6

About the cover: This watercolor, *Portrait of Henry B. Little, with Studies of Hands*, was painted by Waldo Peirce (1884-1970). It was signed on 14 January 1952 and inscribed, "To Mrs. Noyes and best wishes, Waldo Peirce." H. B. Little's daughters, Mrs. Driver, Mrs. Baker, and Mrs. Noyes, presented the painting on December 16, 1980, to J. H. P. ("Hack") Pramberg. In 2005, Mrs. J. H. "Noreen" Pramberg donated the portrait to the Newburyport Public Library. (Permission for the use of the portrait is from the estate of Waldo Peirce from Karin Peirce, daughter of Waldo Peirce, and courtesy of the Newburyport Public Library Archival Center.)

Books on Newburyport, Massachusetts, by Margaret Peckham Motes

Butcher, Baker, Candlestick Maker
Occupations in Newburyport, Massachusetts
from the 1850 Census

Migration to South Carolina:
Movement from the New England and Mid-Atlantic States,
1850 Census

North End Papers
1618-1880
Newburyport, Massachusetts
Development of the North End of the City

Reminiscences of Newburyport
Peter Fudge
An 18th Century Boy

Works Co-Authored with Jesse "Skip" H. Motes

Newburyport Art Association
First Sixty Years
1949-2008

Harbor Range Lights
Newburyport, Massachusetts

PREFACE

HENRY BAILEY LITTLE
1851-1957

"Newburyport Mayor Henry Graf, Jr. wrote the following eulogy on the death of Henry Bailey Little, August 15, 1957:

> *The passing of Henry Bailey Little, the city's oldest citizen and the nation's oldest banker, can be considered the closing of an era that spanned two centuries. During his long lifetime, Mr. Little witnessed four wars and tremendous changes in the American way of life. I feel that his death ends the city's link with the historic past. It is difficult to realize that Mr. Little was not only an eye witness but a part of the events recorded in the histories of Newburyport, and that we now consider as having transpired beyond man's memory.*

The articles written by Henry Bailey Little on his memories of Newburyport were published in August 1959 in the *Newburyport Daily News*, Newburyport, Massachusetts, during Newburyport's 2nd Yankee

Homecoming. They were edited by his daughters, Mrs. Robert M. Driver and Mrs. Charles D. Baker, Jr., as a tribute to their father on the second anniversary of his death.

Some of his papers are in the collections of the Museum of Old Newbury and the Newburyport Public Library Archival Center. Those in the museum's collection are undated, typed manuscripts with pages annotated by his daughters.

These articles have been transcribed from the *Newburyport Daily News* by myself, Margaret "Marge" (Peckham) Motes, with the support of my husband, Jesse Hogan "Skip" Motes, to make them available once again to the public.

I am sure that Mr. Little would be proud to know that his great-grandson, Charles Duane Baker, Jr., was elected as the 72nd Governor of the Commonwealth of Massachusetts, and is now serving his second term.

Marge Motes
April 2019

ACKNOWLEDGMENTS

A special thank you to my husband, Skip Motes, for assistance in reading the text, his suggestions, scanning, and especially for the time I took away from other Newburyport books. Richard K. Lodge, Editor, *Newburyport News*, gave permission to reprint the H. B. Little articles from *The Daily News* during the 2nd Yankee Homecoming. A special thank you to William Peirce, grandson of Waldo Peirce, for the use of the photograph of the artist by Michael Peirce. And thanks especially to Karin Peirce, daughter of Waldo Peirce, for her permission from the estate of Waldo Peirce for the use of the portrait of Henry Bailey Little that is used on the cover of this monograph.

Without the timely article on Waldo Peirce in the spring 2019 issue of the Newburyport Magazine by Will Broaddus, staff writer at the North of Boston Media Group, I would not have known how to contact William "Will" Peirce, the artist's grandson, or family members. His article provided a new understanding of the artist's career and his close friends in Newburyport. Sharon Spieldenner, staff librarian and archivist of the Newburyport Public Library Archival Center, provided help with the H. B. Little papers and photographs from their collection. A thank you also goes to Bethany Groff Dorau, North Shore Regional Site Manager for Historic New England and the Spencer-Pierce-Little farm, for her interest in this project. The farm is where Henry Bailey Little grew up in Newbury, Massachusetts.

Ghlee Woodworth, Newburyport historian, as always helped with ideas from her award winning book on Oak Hill Cemetery, *Tiptoe Through the Tombstones, Oak Hill Cemetery*. Her handwritten map made it an easy drive to find the gravesite of Henry B. Little and his wife, Fanny. My gratitude to Susan Edwards, Director of the Museum of Old Newbury, and Emily Shafer Lawrence, Assistant Director, for their help providing photographs of Newbury and the Little Papers in their collection. Les Ferlazzo provided the history of the Fortnightly Club of which Mr. Little had been a charter member. Mary Anne Clancy, Vice-President of Communications at the Institution for Savings, provided information on Mr. Little's long tenure as the bank's president. To Claire Harper, I am especially grateful for her excellent photography, graphic design of this monograph, and especially for her time, advice, proofreading and patience.

TABLE OF CONTENTS

Preface		vii
Acknowledgments		ix
Table of Contents		xi
Chapter 1	Henry Bailey Little, 1851-1957	1
Chapter 2	Memories of Newburyport, Massachusetts	7
Chapter 3	Some Recollections of a Long Life	9
Chapter 4	Newburyport Shipping as I Remember	17
Chapter 5	Business and Banking	27
Chapter 6	Some Newburyport Citizens	35
Chapter 7	Some of the Seafaring Men Whom I Remember	43
Chapter 8	Some of the Seafaring Men Whom I Remember	49
Chapter 9	Commentaries on Henry B. Little in 1956	55
Chapter 10	Obituary and Tributes to the Life of Henry Bailey Little	61
Addendum I	Mr. Little on the Mayors of Newburyport	73
Addendum II	Newburyport As I Knew It	77
Addendum III	Oldest Bank President, 99, Proud Boast of Newburyport	83
Addendum IV	Waldo Pierce, Artist, 1884-1970	89
Index		93
About the Author		103

Chapter 1

HENRY BAILEY LITTLE, 1851-1957

Henry Bailey Little was born January 3, 1851, in Newbury, Massachusetts, son of Edward Henry Little and Catherine A. (Adams) Little.[1] He was the great-great-grandson of Nicholas Noyes, one of the First Settlers of Newbury. His father, Edward, a well known farmer in Newbury, purchased the Spencer-Pierce home (now the Spencer-Pierce-Little Farm on Little's Lane, Newbury, Massachusetts), between the years 1861 and 1862.[2] The farm consisted of 270 acres and stayed in the Little family for 108 years. The farm and home were gifted by the nieces of Henry Bailey Little, Amelia and Agnes Little, to the Society for the Preservation of New England Antiquities (now Historic New England) in 1969.[3]

Henry grew up on the farm, living with his parents and siblings until his marriage to Fanny Gray in 1878.[4] He and Fanny were the parents of nine children, of whom six survived childhood.[5]

Between 1870-1871, Henry was a clerk at the First National Bank, which later became the First and Ocean National Bank in Newburyport, Massachusetts. He served as director of the bank and the director of the First National Bank of Ipswich.[6]

Spencer-Pierce-Little House, 5 Little's Lane, Newbury, Massachusetts. Photograph by Claire Harper – March 20, 2019.

In 1873, Elisha P. Dodge, Wm. H. Swasey, and Henry B. Little purchased land on Pleasant Street in Newburyport, opposite Inn Street, for a shoe factory. The building was four stories high and said to be the largest brick building built in the city in 30 years. In 1877, Swasey and Sherrill withdrew, leaving the business to E. P. Dodge and Mr. Little. Henry became the treasurer of E. P. Dodge Mfg. Co. in 1898.[7]

Institution for Savings president, Henry B. Little, 1920.[8]
Courtesy of the Newburyport Public Library Archival Center.

At the retirement of Mr. Edward Strong Moseley, president of the Institution for Savings, Newburyport, Massachusetts, Mr. Little became the Institution's 8th president in 1899. He held the position for 54 years, retiring in 1953 at the age of 102.[9]

"Active politically, Mr. Little served on the school committee, the old common council, the city council, the board of assessors, and as a commissioner of the sinking fund. He ran for congress from the Sixth district in 1892 and 1894 and for secretary of state for Massachusetts on the Democratic ticket in 1904.

"Among the numerous offices he held were those of a director of the American Unitarian Association, Treasurer of the First Religious Society of Newburyport, president of the Newburyport Institution for Savings, director of the First and Ocean National Bank, First National Bank of Ipswich of which institution he was the founder and the first president; and treasurer of the Anna Jaques hospital, which institution was of great personal interest to him."[10]

He also served as president of the Anna Jaques Hospital, president of the Historical Society of Old Newbury (now Museum of Old Newbury), on the Newburyport school committee, and with the Society for the Prevention of Cruelty to Animals.

He was very involved in the community and wrote about his memories of life on a farm, now called the Spencer-Pierce-Little Farm, the early days of shipping, merchants, sea captains, business, banking, and covering life in Newburyport, which were published after his death.

A description of Mr. Little appeared in his 1923 passport application when he and wife, Fanny, made a grand tour to Madeira, Azores, Lisbon, Portugal, Paris, Italy, Greece, Egypt, Algeria, and Morocco. He was described as: Age, 72; Height, 5'10 1/2"; Forehead, high; Eyes, blue; Nose, straight; Mouth, straight; Chin, round; Hair, gray; Completion, ruddy; Face, oval.[11]

Fanny (Gray) Little, age 54, died in Newburyport in 1927.

Henry Bailey Little, age 106, died in Newburyport at the Anna Jaques Hospital on August 15, 1957. He was thought to be the oldest bank president in the country when he died. Mr. Little and his wife, Fanny, are buried in Oak Hill Cemetery in Newburyport, Massachusetts.

---

[1] Town of Newbury, Massachusetts Vital Records. p. 199. Ancestry.com. Massachusetts, Birth Records, 1840-1915 (database on-line).

[2] *Southern Essex District Registry of Deeds*: Book 628:240; Book 631:111-112; Book 634:7.

[3] *Southern Essex District Registry of Deeds*: Book 5747:798. Amelia W. Little and Agnes L. Little to The Society for the Preservation of New England Antiquities.

[4] Ancestry.com. Massachusetts, Town and Vital Records, 1620-1988 (database on-line). Newburyport Vital Records. p. 36.

[5] 1910 (NARA microfilm publication T624, 1,178 rolls). Newburyport, MA.

[6] Woodworth, Ghlee. *Tiptoe Through the Tombstones, Oak Hill Cemetery, Vol. 1*. pub. 2008. p. 44.

[7] *Newburyport and Amesbury City Directory.* Pub.1898. p. 100.

[8] *Century of the Institution for Savings In Newburyport and its Vicinity, 1820-1920.* Pub. 1920. Institution for Savings.

[9] Email from Mary Anne Clancy, Institution for Savings, Newburyport, Massachusetts, March 26, 2018. "He was the eighth president. The bank will celebrate its 200th anniversary in 2020."

[10] *Newburyport Daily News*, "Passing of Henry Bailey Little Recalls Service to Community." August 16, 1957.

[11] Series Title: "Passenger Lists of Vessels Arriving at Boston, Massachusetts, 1891-1943." The National Archives at Washington, D.C.; Washington, D.C.: Record Group: 85; Series Number: T843; NARA Roll Number: 416.

Chapter 2

MEMORIES OF NEWBURYPORT, MASSACHUSETTS

BY HENRY BAILEY LITTLE

Published in the *Newburyport Daily News*
During the Second Yankee Homecoming

August 1959

The Henry Bailey Little Papers from the collection of the Museum of Old Newbury are manuscripts by H. B. Little which were transcribed by his daughters, Mrs. Josephine M. Driver and Mrs. Charles D. Baker, Jr., for publication in the *Newburyport Daily News* in August 1959. He was a charter member of the Fortnightly Club, and some of his papers on Newburyport can be found at the Museum of Old Newbury and the Newburyport Public Library Archival Center.

Chapter 3

SOME RECOLLECTIONS OF A LONG LIFE

BY HENRY BAILEY LITTLE

"Editor's note: We are pleased to publish the first in a series of articles today, written by the late Henry Bailey Little, who died aged 106, and edited by his daughters Mrs. Robert M. Driver and Mrs. Charles D. Baker, Jr. We consider the series timely in view of the current celebration of Homecoming in this city."

August 1959

"I was born January 3, 1851 in Newbury. My father was a well-to-do farmer who first rented and then bought the ancient house known as the 'Garrison House' or the 'Spencer-Pierce House.'[1] Architecturally, I am told, that it is interesting, but we merely thought of it as an ordinary dwelling.

"The first thing which I remember, for which I can give a definite date, is when I was three years old, I attended my aunt's and uncle's wedding. What impressed me then was the fact that I rode in a hack -- it was the first time I had ever been in a closed carriage.

"The first event of public interest that I remember is the talk I heard in reference to the hanging of John Brown. Here was a criminal who would have been convicted by any jury in any State in the Union, but, in less than three years, people were singing 'John Brown's Body' and he was considered a martyr. I do not think the present generation can feel or understand the intense feeling of that time. I have understood that, in one household of my family connection, a fast was kept on the day Brown was hanged.

"**The Presidential election of 1860 is impressed on my memory as being the first time I ever witnessed a torch-light parade.** The Wide-awakes, as they were called, supporters of Lincoln, marched through the streets. I also remember the ballot used at that time, as on it appeared the names of John A. Andrews for Governor and John I. Baker, the mild-eyed sage of Beverly, who was a candidate for the Governor's Council. My first realization of the Civil War was the Battle of Bull Run and I could not comprehend Union defeat, as I thought the Northern troops would march directly to Richmond. I saw something of the mustering of the troops and I remember an encampment of soldiers in Lynnfield, which my father took me to see, but I have no very distinct remembrance of the course of the war until the Battle of Antietam. Captain Bartlett of a local company was killed there and I had seen him crossing State Street in uniform only a short time before. I received news of President Lincoln's assassination while driving an oak cart in Newburyport. Naturally a boy of 14 would get a severe shock and it was hard for me to reconcile myself.

"**In my span of life so many changes have come about that it amounts to a social revolution.** Today it is doubtful if there is one family in 10 who could go for 48 hours without sending to the bakery or grocery store for supplies. My father's family, with the help who boarded on the place, numbered not less than 12 people. To provide for them he purchased molasses, flour, and pilot bread by the barrel, tea by the chest, raisins by the box (or crate), salted mackerel in various sizes, by the half-barrel, hams, packed in salt hay, filled another barrel. Cheese was treated the same way. When freezing weather came, he purchased a quarter of beef, which was utilized as required, and he also bought 50 or 60 pounds of sausages. In the cellar would be 2 barrels of salt pork raised on the place, and a barrel of corned beef. Likewise in the cellar would be all the vegetables necessary to carry the family through the winter. Baldwin apples for the winter season and russets for the spring, the latter often holding good until July. I do not think granulated sugar existed in my father's day. The only white sugar was the loaf variety from which one cut or broke off small pieces.

"Sometimes my father had tenants (60 or more) who took from 1/4 acre to an acre of land on which they raised vegetables. These tenants were largely laborers about the wharves who were busy only when working on the cargoes of coasters. Farm wages for the ordinary help, about the time of the Civil War, were $8.00 a month and board for the three winter months and $14.00 a month and board for the rest of the year.

"**In my young days, central heating, as it is called, was scarcely known.** In the winter 2 or 3 rooms in a house would be heated with cast-iron stoves; but the main part would be at the temperature of the outside world. It would be no unusual matter for the water to freeze in the sleeping-rooms pitchers and bowls. Again, as a matter of housekeeping, lighting was done by candles or whale-oil lamps, while the town itself was in darkness. This method was succeeded about 1865, by kerosene lamps. The gas-plant was installed in my day, but I remember but little about it, as only a small portion of the city was covered. Now every house is so equipped that pressing a button gives all the illumination required.

"One of the greatest changes between my day and the present is in transportation. If a young man wished to take his best girl out for an airing, a ten mile ride with a horse and buggy would be the limit of the trip. Now he can take her to the mountains for lunch and still be at home in good season.

"Also there is a considerable saving of time in communication. In early days the postage to California was 25 cents and it would be three or four months before you could get an answer to a letter. Now you can step to the telephone and in ten minutes, can conclude a business deal with San Francisco.

"**Another revolution is in the matter of dress.** As a schoolboy in High School, I remember that one of the pupils wore short dresses, otherwise all the girls wore long skirts and were mortified if accidentally they should show an ankle. For head dresses they wore hats or bonnets, often with long veils, enclosing their heads. Their faces only being exposed. Today girls of the same age have bare legs and dresses scarcely to their knees. Their heads are uncovered, unless they wear handkerchiefs, which, in my younger days, were only permissible if the lady was going to the clothes-line or to work in the flower-garden. As for the male sex, boys always wore hats, wide-brimmed straw in summer and a sort of flat derby in the winter. The business man attended to his affairs in a long-tailed coat or a Prince Albert and frequently wore a tall silk hat. Most men had beards or at least mustaches, and some sported 'Dundrearies,' which were side-whiskers.

"I remember when there were only four people in town who kept a pair of horses for driving purposes (The two Baileys, Dr. Kelly, who lived at the Dexter house, and Mrs. Henry Wills) and perhaps fifteen who had one driving horse, used for pleasure rather than business. Now there are over a thousand automobiles in the city. As a predecessor to the automobile, Frank Curtis had a steam wagon which he brought on the street several times, but it so frightened the horses that he was obliged to give it up. Later he sold it to Dr. Dimmick, a dentist, who left Newburyport eventually, and went to the West Indies. The steam wagon was stored for many years in the Harris Street Livery Stable. I wonder what became of it.

"After the Civil War there were 2 militia companies in town, both belonging to the Eighth Regiment, and they continued for many years. Why they disbanded I never knew. I remember when the First Brigade of the Massachusetts militia encamped down on the Kelly Field in Oldtown, which was named for the first settler who came north of Oldtown Hill and, incidentally, was one of my ancestors. The place is still called the Kelly Field.

"There was also an artillery company in town which was composed of middle-aged men. It has no connection with the militia and probably existed for the purpose of showing off their uniforms occasionally. The first captain I remember was Captain Burrill and he was succeeded by Judge Currier. The last captain was Johnny McCusker.

"**There were eight fire-engine companies,** all machines being hand-tubs, one, Number 4, being out of commission in my recollection. Every year the department had a try-out to see which company would attain the silver trumpet for the ensuing year. The play-out was held on Green Street, the engine being at the reservoir near Washington, and probably threw 200 feet of hose down [the] street.

"What little education I received came from the Putnam Free School, a High school which, by the terms of the Putnam will, did not teach dead languages. Mine was the last class, but one to graduate. It was then, in some manner, consolidated with the Newburyport High

School, but at present the income (the Putnam Fund) is used to further the education for individual pupils in technical, college courses."

Henry Bailey Little stands with Judge Harlan Fiske Stone in 1945 at the 50th Reunion of the Putnam Free School, Class of 1895.
Courtesy of the Museum of Old Newbury.

---

[1] *Southern Essex District Registry of Deeds*: Book 268:240, Book 631:111-112, Book 634:7 "Edward H. Little purchased the property from the heirs of the (John) Pettingell family in 1861; at the time of the purchase, Little had been a tenant on the property for approximately ten years..." (From Bethany Groff Dorau, Historic New England, North Shore Site Manager, Spencer-Pierce-Little Farm.)

Putnam Free School, High Street, Newburyport, Massachusetts. Courtesy of the Museum of Old Newbury, Snow Photograph Collection.

Chapter 4

NEWBURYPORT SHIPPING AS I REMEMBER

BY HENRY BAILEY LITTLE

"Editor's note: This is the second in a series of papers written some years ago by the Newburyport banker-historian Henry Bailey Little, who died in 1957 at the age of 106. The papers were made available to the Daily News by his family for publication this Yankee Homecoming Week."

August 4, 1959

"With the exception of the cotton mills, practically all the business of the town was on the river-bank, the shipyards, and the wharves. The shipyards have disappeared and been forgotten and the wharves are in a state of decay. The last square-rigger was built here in 1884 and while there were a few small vessels built later, after that date shipbuilding was for the most part ended.

"The wharves were busy places with lumber and coal-yards and sheds where fish was packed. As late as 1874 there were 33 vessels engaged in the Banks and Labrador fishing, for cod and mackerel. David and Isaac Hale, who owned the City (just off Market square) and Central wharves, had their counting room on the second floor of the building at the end of City wharf. We had counting-rooms, in those days, not offices. The Hales had quite a fleet of coasters with their names all beginning with the letter H ---- the Halo, the Huntress, the Hiawatha, the Heron and several others.

"Robert Bailey [Bayley] and Sons,[2] who occupied the building recently utilized by Yerxa and Company, had a wharf adjoining which always seemed to be covered with hogsheads of molasses, which I presume, went largely to the Caldwells for the manufacture of rum.

"In the report of a heavy snowstorm which took place in my young days, the Newburyport Herald, in its next issue, stated that of the 102 vessels in port, several were damaged and one was sunk at the wharf. At another time, the paper reported that 'It was a grand sight yesterday when 40 sail put to sea, after being storm-bound in the harbor for a week.'

"**It is curious to note that none of the full-rigged ships that were built here ever returned,** although many of them entered Boston harbor. They were principally in the China and Calcutta trade. Among later ones built here were the 'Importer,' the 'Exporter,' and the 'Reporter,' all managed by Sumner, Swasey and Currier who occupied the building now owned by Swift and Company. In those days, before the City Railroad was inaugurated, the docks

---

[2] Robert Bailey and Sons located on Water Street is now the home of the Newburyport Art Association.

Sign for Yerxa's Groceries at 63 Water Street (today 65 Water Street). Courtesy of the Newburyport Public Library Archival Center, Bill Lane Collection of Newburyport and Vicinity, 1964-2000.

The Jackman Ropewalk on Marlboro Street, in Newbury (now a part of Newburyport), MA, circa 1870, was demolished in 1899. Shipyards employed a variety of skilled tradesmen, rope makers among them, producing thousands of feet of specialized rope called cordage, used to rig each sailing vessel. Rope makers worked in wooden sheds, 400 to 1000 feet in length, called ropewalks. One workman would walk strands down the length of the shed while another operated a spinner at one end, twisting the strands into rope. Courtesy of the Museum of Old Newbury.

came right up to Water street and the traffic on the street went on under the overhanging bowsprits.

"**In those days quite a fleet of schooners went regularly to the Labrador Coast,** fishing for cod, and when the cargoes were received in Newburyport, the fish was cured on fish-flakes which covered acres of ground on lower Water Street. There were also several boats fishing for mackerel, which were packed in kegs on shore.

"The decline of the West Indies trade was very gradual. The last ship from there arrived August 16, 1877, with a cargo of sugar. The business of the wharves also disappeared gradually, the last arrival being just before World War 2 when a Nova Scotia vessel delivered a cargo of wood.

"**During the time of ship building, we also had a number of rope walks.** I remember five: two on Bromfield Street, two on Marlborough and one on Chestnut. These were rough buildings hundreds of feet long. Another help to shipping was the bakery of Pearson and Butler, who furnished crackers and hard biscuits, the latter usually referred to as hard tack, for the crews. My father always had a barrel of Butler's biscuits on hand and, in summer, the men on the farm used to be given hard tack and milk for their luncheons.

"One very specialized trade was that of the riggers. After a ship's hull was launched, the masts, spars, standing and running rigging had to be placed, triced, and trigged. As the sailors themselves understood such operations, many of them worked at this job when ashore. Capt. Oliver Jones gives an excellent idea of this work in his reminiscences.

"He says, 'I was working in the **Pritchard** rigging gang and it was the only time in my sea life when I was earning two salaries, $60 per month gold, as mate and $2 per day in the rigging gang. This gang was one of the institutions of Newburyport as the men rigged all the ships that were built here, from the launching of the ship to the final departure to some port. Every detail was entrusted to their care and, at times, they furnished the men to take the ship around to Boston or New York for loading. The men were such experts that their services were often asked for in places other than Newburyport. The business (or rather craft) was frequently handed down in a family from father to son to grandson, until shipbuilding received its final blow by the outbreak of the Civil War. Nearly all our Newburyport shipmasters, in their early days, have worked in the rigging gang while at home between voyages.'

"**As late as 1873 the customs receipts were $59,464. Arrivals and departures noted 1,219 vessels.** In 1874 there were 98 registered vessels owned wholly or in part in this customs district and at the same time there were, in process of construction, 4 ships, 1 barque, and 4 schooners. Many of the ships built in Newburyport were commanded by Newburyport shipmasters."

Pritchard Company workmen (a "rigging gang") are installing running and standing rigging on the new ship, *Daniel I. Tenney*, at Bayley's Wharf in 1875. Photograph by Selwyn Reed.
Courtesy of Scott Nason.

The schooner, *Edward Lemeyer*, unloads hogsheads of sugar and molasses imported from the West Indies onto Robert Bayley's wharf on Water Street, Newburyport, MA, c. 1875. Carte de visite photograph by Carl Meinerth. Courtesy of the Museum of Old Newbury, Snow Photograph Collection.

West Indies hogsheads of sugar and molasses are staged on Bayley's Wharf, waiting to be stored in a bonded warehouse after Customs' inspection. Note the Newburyport City Railroad tracks. The brig, *Tula*, and schooner, *Edward Lemeyer*, are tied up at the foot of the wharf.
Courtesy of the Museum of Old Newbury, Snow Photograph Collection.

Chapter 5

BUSINESS AND BANKING

BY HENRY BAILEY LITTLE

"Editor's note: This is the third in a series of papers written some years ago by the Newburyport banker-historian Henry Bailey Little, who died in 1957 at age of 106. The papers were made available to the Daily News by his family for publication this Yankee Homecoming week."

August 5, 1959

"About two weeks after I graduated from high school, I became the messenger of the First National bank[3] -- such a character does not exist at the present time. My duties took me from the shipyards at the north end of town to Joppa and the Newbury line. At this time the bank was on the north side of State street, nearly down to Market Square. This position I held from the time I was 16 until I was 21.

FIRST NATIONAL BANK,

NO. 16 STATE STREET,

ORGANIZED FEBRUARY, 1864.

CAPITAL, ...$300,000.

CHARLES H. COFFIN, President.

T. B. STICKNEY, Cashier.

DIRECTORS:

CHARLES H. COFFIN,
EBEN SUMNER,
HENRY COOK,
ROBERT COUCH,
WILLIAM THURSTON,
EDWARD P. SHAW,
AMOS COFFIN,
HENRY B. LITTLE,
TIMOTHY REMICK.

First National Bank Advertisement.
Newburyport City Directory, 1880.
Courtesy of the Newburyport Public Library Archival Center.

---

[3] *Newburyport City Directory for the year ending October 1919*, pp. 504-506. By 1919, Henry B. Little was director of the First National Bank, located at 16 State Street, director of the Ocean Bank at 51 State Street, and president of the Institution for Savings at 81 State Street.

"During this period there were four commercial banks in Newburyport, with a combined capital of $770,000. The staff of each bank consisted of three persons, a cashier, a bookkeeper, and a messenger boy, the latter a necessity, as of course, this was before the days of telephones. I do not presume that all four banks together did as much business as one of the present banks. Very few people, in my young days, had checking accounts -- now everyone seems to need one.

"What of the local savings banks? There were then two, as at present, The Institution for Savings[4] is the third established in the state, only Boston and Salem having preceded it. The date of the opening for business was April 5, 1820. The bank was originally located in the selectmen's rooms, though most of its business was transacted in the office of Jeremiah Nelson who was treasurer for 11 years. At first office hours were one hour each week and daily service was not rendered until the bank had been running 25 years. In its years of existence it has also occupied space in an insurance office at the corner of State and Pleasant streets; then to the second floor of the building at the corner of State and Essex streets. In my early recollections it was over the Merchant's bank. The site of the present building was originally occupied by a livery stable before the bank was built in 1872. The bank was enlarged and remodeled in 1904.

---

[4] The Institution for Savings was chartered on January 31, 1820. It was the third savings bank in the commonwealth, and its incorporators established the bank "for the purpose of receiving money on deposit and investing the same to the best advantage of the owners thereof." Opening deposits totaling $463.10 were collected the first day. (Museum of Old Newbury)

The Institution for Savings at 93 State Street, Newburyport, Massachusetts, c. 1918. Courtesy of the Museum of Old Newbury, Snow Photograph Collection.

"I personally remember one of the incorporators, Edward S. Rand. William B. Bannister, the first president lived in what is now the Dalton club next door.

"**I remember very well when he [we] had five cotton mills** -- one in a frame building situated just above the bridge across the river. It made a great impression on me, as it was the first large building I ever saw illuminated. Called the Essex Cotton Mill, it was destroyed by fire when I was quite young. The other cotton mills were the Ocean on Munroe street, the James on Salem street, and the Globe, which extended south from the upper side of Federal street. This was later taken down. The Bartlet Mill, at the corner of Pleasant and Inn streets, burned much to the satisfaction of the stock holders. While the fire was raging I spent most of the time on the top of our shoe factory (opposite) counting the cinders. Another mill was simply abandoned.

"At one time there was a yarn mill on Tracy place, which made the cotton yarns for hosiery, but the mill only lasted for a few years.

"**In my early recollection there was one small shoe factory on Merrimac Street,** and during my banking experience, another small one started on the upper floor of a building near lower State street.

"Neither of these firms employed more than 20 persons. Later a three-story building on the corner of Hale's Court and Pleasant Street, was occupied by two shoe-firms, one of which (the Dodge factory), erected the building on Pleasant Street, which was later continued through into Prince Place. Other factories were built afterwards and shoe manufacturing became the principal activity of the town.

"**Silverware was made in a small way, for several generations.** I remember three firms that were in this business, and one, which was located in the Dodge shoe factory, was the predecessor of the present Towle company. Other industries have been started from time to time. I remember machine shops, comb shops, hat brush and paper collar making, arms making, and the manufacture of trolley cars.

"All general business was conducted by small concerns. In the early 70s there were over 60 grocers in the city who mostly ran family-staffed neighborhood stores."

The Globe Steam Mills, Water Street, Newburyport, Massachusetts. Courtesy of Robert Currier.

Dodge Brothers Shoe Company, at the Corner of Prince Place and State Street, Newburyport, Massachusetts. Courtesy of the Museum of Old Newbury, Snow Photograph Collection.

Chapter 6

SOME NEWBURYPORT CITIZENS

BY HENRY BAILEY LITTLE

"Editor's note: This is the fourth in a series of papers written some years ago by the Newburyport banker, historian Henry Bailey Little, who died in 1957 at the age of 106. The papers were made available to the Daily News by his family."

August 6, 1959

"**William H. Swasey** was a member of the firm of Sumner, Swasey, and Currier, largely interested in shipping and wholesale dealing in groceries, produce, etc. After retiring from that firm, he was for years the treasurer of the Towle Manufacturing company. In his later years, Mr. Swasey used to state that we now taught in the schools what he was thrashed for doing, in his day. He became something of an amateur artist -- a talent which had evidently not been properly appreciated when he practiced it in his school-days -- and fitted up a room in his house for the purpose of executing still lifes and landscapes. He was an excellent craftsman, but perhaps his painting would not be called a great success. At his death his fortune was distributed largely among charitable and religious organizations.

"**William Cushing** was the half-brother of Caleb Cushing. He was associated with his father in the shipping business and in early life went to the Pacific Coast for some little time, representing the Cushing interests there. He was for three years mayor of the city, also president of the Ocean bank, and at the last of his life occupied the house at 63 High street, formerly the Burnhome estate.

"**Eben F. Stone** was a prominent lawyer, president of the first City Council, mayor of the city, and colonel of the 48th Massachusetts regiment in the Civil War. He represented the Essex District in Congress for three terms, and also served many times in the Massachusetts Legislature, both in the House and the Senate. The latter part of his life he lived in the house on the corner of State and Greenleaf streets.

"**Edward S. Moseley** was an able and successful man of business; in all his business life he was interested in shipping. He was president of the Institution for Savings and also of the Mechanics National Bank. He was a man of strong personality and great self-confidence, at times rather arrogant. At one time, when instructed by the board of investment of the Institution for Savings to invest the surplus funds in anything he thought desirable with the exception of United States bonds, he visited Boston and purchased $100,000 of said bonds and nothing else! However, the bank owed much to his excellent management and forethought.

"**Charles H. Coffin** was a man of a larger variety of business experience than often comes to the lot of anyone. Before he was of age he was owner of a dry goods store on State street, opposite Essex street and, while there, laid the first brick sidewalk in Newburyport. At the time of the gold excitement in California, he bought a ship, paid $5 on account, collected the passage money and advances on the freights and, when the ship arrived in San Francisco, he owned her. He was the first president of the First National bank, which he helped to organize, and was interested at different times in many classes of business. He was not always successful in his ventures, and on two occasions was obliged to suspend payments, but, as I learned from the old cashier of the bank, he always paid in full finally.

"**Rev. Daniel T. Fiske** was for a long time pastor of the Belleville church. He had a very gracious personality, was an easy speaker and was much beloved by his parishioners, as well as being respected by all. He was more liberal in his views perhaps than most of the orthodox clergy of his day, and was a trustee for a time, of the Andover Theological Seminary.

"**Warren Currier** was a member of the firm of Sumner, Swasey and Currier to which reference has already been made. At its dissolution he moved to New York and was for years with the Cunard Steamship company. When ill health compelled him to resign that position, he returned to Newburyport where he lived in the house now occupied by Miss Lorna Learned.

"**Philip K. Hills** was a man of remarkable personality, one of the easiest and best impromptu speakers that I have ever known. He was always interested in politics and active in the party meetings and conventions, also a member of the city government and the school board at various times. As a very young man he was [a] clerk in the Ocean National bank which he left to become secretary of the Institution of Savings and later its treasurer. During the last of his life he was totally blind, but always cheerful and extremely entertaining with his reminiscences. He was the father of the celebrated painter, Miss Laura

Hills, and in his house on the upper corner of Washington and Market streets, he had a studio arranged for her on the third floor.

"**Nathan Noyes Withington,** the son of the Rev. Leonard Withington, was in early life a teacher. He spent a number of years in Missouri, and, at the time of the breaking out of the Civil War, he stated later, he knew he should be obliged to take part, but on which side, he was for a long time, unable to decide. He finally entered the Union Army in the 11th Massachusetts Infantry, was partially disabled, and served for the remainder of the war in the Veterans' Reserve Corps. He was admitted to the bar after the war, but practiced very little as he then became, and was for years, the editor of the Newburyport Herald, for which he wrote easy and voluminous articles. In a district convention in the early 70s he came within one vote of being nominated as a candidate for Congress, which, if successful, would have meant a certainty of election. This defeat was attributed to one of his own townsmen, with whom he had had some contention.

"**Jacob Stone** was for some time the cashier of the Ocean National Bank. At the breaking out of the Civil War the management of the bank was so 'coppery' (or Southern in sympathy) that it was quite disagreeable to Mr. Stone and some of his customers, so he sent in his resignation. His friends immediately organized the First National Bank of which he became cashier and where he served until his death. I served under him as a clerk in the bank. Mr. Stone, although a man of decided convictions, was a very quiet, slow-spoken man, and of a gracious personality.

"**Amos Noyes** was a most eccentric individual and difficult to understand. Although he had no sense of humor, he would at times convulse his hearers by his unusual, really unique speech. In any discussion he was perfectly capable of taking a point of view entirely foreign to his belief and to argue it as readily as if thoroughly convinced he was right. So absent minded was he that, on the first Sunday after his marriage, he went to his old home on Essex street after church, leaving his wife -- a stranger in town -- to find her way home as best she could. At another time, after consulting some client in his law office, he walked out and locked the door. The client had to shout from the window for a ladder to be brought for his rescue. Mr. Noyes was the first United States assessor under the Internal Revenue Act of Civil War days and he also served some years on the school board.

"**John James Currier** was the son of John Currier, Jr., the noted shipbuilder. He was associated with his father for many years, was treasurer of the Bailey Hat Company, served in both branches of the city government and was likewise mayor. He will be remembered by the public for his four volumes of history covering 'Ould Newbury.' Had he lived, there would probably have been an additional volume, as he informed me that he had enough material for one. Mr. Currier was quite slight of physique, but that did not prevent him from expressing his views most emphatically to much more imposing men. On one occasion, when he visited the Herald office, Senator Sargent of California was present. As Mr. Huse, the proprietor, introduced the two men, Senator Sargent extended his hand in greeting -- but Mr. Currier put both hands behind him and very warmly said 'I take no man by the hand who was guilty of defeating Caleb Cushing for Chief Justice.' Unfortunately, history does not record the reactions of the Senator and Mr. Huse.

"**Dr. Francis A. Howe** was a physician living on the corner of High and Carter streets. He came to Newburyport in the late 1850s and for many years was known as 'the young doctor.' I presume that at some time in conversation with Miss Anna Jaques, he had expressed his view on the need of a hospital in Newburyport, for, when he was making a professional visit, she went to an adjoining room and returned with $25,000 in Massachusetts State bonds, handed them to him and requested him to start his hospital. Dr. Howe became the first president of the hospital, a position he held until his death.

"**James Parton** was born in Canterbury, England, almost in the shadow of its cathedral, in spite of which ecclesiastical beginning, he always declared himself to be an atheist, although no one who knew him would believe this to be a proper designation. In early days he was a journalist, but later devoted himself to other forms of writing, much of which was biographical. The first of his works was, I believe, <u>The Life of Benjamin F. Butler</u>. He was very positive in his ideas, some of which were not in keeping with the popular views of the town. On hearing a paper given by Mr. E. P. Dodge, concerning the protective tariff, he remarked 'It was the best defense of an indefensible plan that he had ever heard.' He was an exceedingly interesting conversationalist and a very decided acquisition to any gathering.

"**Robert Toppan** lived only briefly in Newburyport, but he was a person of marked individuality, so much so that those who met him never forgot him. He married a Newburyport girl, Sarah M. Cushing, daughter of William Cushing. Mr. Toppan was the son of Charles Toppan, one of the organizers of the American Banknote Company. Robert Toppan spent much of his time in Europe and was a fine linguist. At the time of the election to the successor to Pope Pius the Ninth, he managed to enter the convention hall of the cardinals before they had adjourned, having secured entrance by joining himself with the attendants of one of the cardinals. He also succeeded in entering Paris at the time of the Commune.

"**Elisha P. Dodge** commenced his business career in Newburyport before he came of age as a shoe manufacturer and continued in this line of business until his death. He was one of those fortunate men who have the facility of doing well whatever they undertake. He was, in his younger days, quite an amateur actor and was always excellent in the parts taken. He was for many years a member of the school board, he was also mayor of the city, president of the Mechanics National bank, and held many other positions of trust.

"**Frank F. Morrill** spent most of his early days in Chattanooga, Tennessee and in Cleveland. At the wish of his father he returned to Amesbury after the latter had retired from business. Not finding a satisfactory residence in Amesbury, he located in Newburyport, although he never engaged in business here. He was a most ready speaker, always having decided views of his own, which were most gracefully expressed.

"**Henry M. Cross,** a native of Newburyport, entered the coal business and later represented the Philadelphia and Reading Coal company here. He was one of the parties who originally introduced the telephone in this city. During the Civil War he became a captain after one enlistment, and was taken prisoner by the Confederate forces. He was confined for a considerable time in one of their military prisons, but he finally escaped with several companions. The latter part of his business career was with the Gamewell Fire Alarm company.

"**Luther Dame** came to Newburyport in 1848 as an instructor in the Putnam Free School. When the Civil War broke out he became a captain in the 11th Massachusetts Regiment, but before that, he was one of the emigrants to Kansas and took part in the pre-war difficulties there. After the war he taught for 20 years in our local High school, retiring only when his failing sight made it necessary.

"**John L. Dodge** was born in Ipswich and became a civil engineer, working on the Erie Canal and the New York railroads. He later went into the shoe business in Troy, but discontinued that and returned to work under Tilden, on the canals. On coming to Newburyport, he became interested in the shoe business, first with his brother, E. P. Dodge, and then with his sons, Chauncey W. and Harry D. Dodge.

"**Joseph E. Moody** learned the trade of cabinet-maker, but enlisted to fight in the Civil War and was sergeant-major of the 48th Regiment, later a lieutenant. He was captured at the same time as Captain Cross and was with him in the Confederate prison. After the war he went to Petersburg, Va. and was, for a short time, in business in that city. Later, and for most of his business life, he was in the wholesale fish business in Boston, and at the time of his death held the record as a commuter between Newburyport and that city.

"**Albert C. Titcomb** was, at the time the Civil War broke out in the jewelry business in Mobile, Ala. Fleeing from confederacy he entered business in San Francisco and later came to Newburyport after his retirement. He became treasurer for a time, of the Lamson Store Service corporation and also served as mayor of the city. At the time of his death he was living in the house now owned by Mr. Richardson (The Colonial Manor).

"**Charles H. Cutting** was born in Vermont, near the Canadian line, where he spent his early childhood. Later he came to Charlestown, where his father was in business and graduated from the Boston Latin High school. While there he frequently acted as a super in Boston theatre and had many interesting acquaintances among the old-time actors and actresses. Where he got his experience as a civil engineer I cannot say, but he was employed as such for some of the Western railroads and was also a railroad contractor. Sometimes, in the winter season, he was a boss of a group of lumber jacks. Later he became a mining engineer and, at the last of his business career, he was a copper miner in Arizona. During a large portion of his life his legal residence was in Minneapolis, but, as he married a Newburyporter, he came here to live on his retirement from active business. He became interested in local affairs and was for a while, president of the Anna Jaques Hospital."

Chapter 7

SOME OF THE SEAFARING MEN WHOM I REMEMBER

BY HENRY BAILEY LITTLE

"Editor's note: This is the fifth in a series of papers written some years ago by the Newburyport banker-historian Henry Bailey Little, who died in 1957 at the age of 106. The papers were made available to the Daily News by his family."

August 7, 1959

"As Newburyport in its prosperity was a sea-faring port and dependent upon shipbuilding and foreign trade, it naturally produced sailors and shipmasters. It is likely that more than half the boys in town went to sea for at least one voyage and many made it a life profession. In my youth many of the men I shall mention here were still active ship-masters, others had retired at that time. But, of them all, I can recall 72 and this means not coastwise skippers, but those engaged in foreign trade.

"The Marine society, which was composed entirely of ship-captains, was a very flourishing organization even in my day. It owned the building at numbers 10 and 12 State Street, the upper floors of which it occupied. The rooms contained a handsome museum housing items collected by the members in foreign lands, and there was also a collection of photographs of many of the later members, which is now, together with the museum pieces, owned by the Historical Society. [Today, they are part of the collections of the Museum of Old Newbury and the Custom House Maritime Museum.]

"At one time, in driving up High Street from Bromfield Street, I pointed out to my companion 22 houses, which in my day had been

Former Marine Society Building with Plaque, State Street, Newburyport, MA.
Photograph by Claire Harper – March 20, 2019.

occupied by shipmasters. I am also aware that four others lived on Boardman Street in the three handsome gambrel-roofed houses on the corners of Boardman and Washington Streets. These men were two Clarksons, Paul Titcomb, and Captain John Simpson.

"My list is an alphabetical one, so I shall begin with Capt. Avery. He was born in Castine, Maine, but lived here for years. He was one of the mariners who suffered shipwreck, having lost the ship J. P. Whitney in a typhoon in the Indian Ocean. He had traded off the coast of Africa and in the East Indies, as well as carrying cotton to England.

"**Of the Browns, I remember five.** Perhaps the best known was Capt. Laurence Brown whose ship was taken and burned by the 'Alabama.' He was set adrift with his crew and passengers being allowed neither food nor water, compass nor chart. However they were rescued and taken to Calcutta. Capt. Brown was very bowlegged and I have heard that a lady visiting here made the remark that she knew he must be an accomplished horseman, as she recognized the build. On being told of this, Capt. Brown is said to have commented that the only thing he was an expert at riding was a vessel's yards.

"This Lawrence Brown was one of eight brothers, all of whom had earned the title of captain. From one of their descendants I have heard the story that from the day the eldest went to sea until the last one died, only on one occasion were they all at home together. On that occasion their mother entertained them at dinner, and she could address each one of them as 'Captain' Brown. There is a fine portrait of Capt. Nicholas Brown, the eldest, hanging in the Historical Society [now the Museum of Old Newbury].

"**Of the Bayleys there were five,** and they had rather a salty air even in the way they spelled their name -- Bayley. Two of them did the principal importing business of the town during my day, which consisted largely of sugar, molasses, and coffee. Their place of business was afterwards occupied by the Victor Manufacturing Company, that building having been their office. They had two of the finest gardens in town, one of them living on Milk Street, the other on Purchase Street, their properties adjoining in the rear.

"**There were four Brays.** Capt. Isaac Bray who built the house on the corner of High and Allen Streets, was the master of the ship Bengal, on which a granddaughter of old Capt. Peter Le Breton and her children sailed from Philadelphia to San Francisco to join the father of the family. A description of the voyage was given in a book called <u>A California Family</u> written by Mrs. George W. Marston of San Diego, one of the children who made the trip.

"(Capt. Brooks and Capt. Balch were both mentioned here, but with no anecdotes or descriptions.)

"**Capt. Bogardus** lived in the house now owned by Mr. Richard Welch, on High Street, just above Kent. He was a native of Russia, I believe, and had strong Southern sympathies, and, at the outbreak of the Civil War, made his neighbors very angry by hanging out a Confederate flag.

"Among the later masters were the two Colbys.

"**Captain Couch,** after he left the sea was mayor of Newburyport, a member of the governor's council, and he also served on the School Committee. During the Civil War he sold his ship in Liverpool. The exchange was largely in his favor and gold was at a high premium, so that I was informed by my father, he became the largest owner of government bonds in the city -- $80,000 worth.

"**Capt. Henry Cook, who lived at the corner of Orange and Federal Streets,** was active in my day, and was one of the early directors of the First National Bank. Two of his sons were sailors. One was lost at sea in the ship 'Black Hawk' and the other died in a hospital in

Liverpool. (Mr. Little does not refer to a story of Capt. Cook's son, which was well-known in Newburyport at that time. Mrs. Cook, looking from her window one day saw her son whom she knew to be at sea, coming up the front walk. She rushed to the door and met him on the steps -- but he only said 'I've come home mother' and then vanished. When she had recovered from her shock somewhat, Mrs. Cook noted down the circumstances of the vision and when a survivor of the wreck on reaching Newburyport, called to tell her the sad facts of her son's death, she knew of the event before he could repeat it. The time of the boy's death coincided with his appearance to his mother.)

"**Captain Cheever was a master who was severely injured by the mutiny of an East Indian sailor** who stabbed one officer to death and wounded two others. The first mate, later captain, Fred Kezer, managed to overcome the Lascar, brought the ship to port and, by his care, saved Capt. Cheever's life. The latter was obliged to give up the sea and, for a long time, was an invalid.

"Of Captains Emerton, Elliott, and Evans, I can say nothing as I have but little remembrance of them; however, Capt. Elliott was for many years in command of the life-saving station at Plum Island.

"There were three Graves captains; Capt. William Graves who was at one time mayor of the city; Capt. Edward Graves who was lost in an Indian Ocean typhoon, and Alexander who was the grandfather of the late Major Perkins. Capt. William was for a long time treasurer of the Bartlet Mills and was always interested in city affairs."

Chapter 8

SOME OF THE SEAFARING MEN WHOM I REMEMBER

BY HENRY BAILEY LITTLE

August 8, 1959

"There were three Hales: George W. Hale, Eliphalet Hale, and Joshua. The latter lived at 300 High street (now belonging to Mr. William Kinsman) and is one of the few captains who has a descendant (This was written before Mr. Josiah Hale died). Capt. Hale went to sea originally, not because it was the profession he had chosen, but to restore his failing health. He started his business life in an insurance office in New York, but found that, for some reason, he was unable to live on shore. He was a successful ship-captain for 15 years and then returned to Newburyport to live, becoming interested in the affairs of the town.

"Of Capt. Hoyt I have a very slight remembrance. Capt. Howard was one of the youngest whom I recall, and was the last captain but one to join the Marine society -- in 1885. His last sailings were from San Francisco.

"**There were three Johnsons,** two of them living where Miss Frances and Richard Johnson live now, in the Tracy house on High Street, and the other living opposite on the corner of Olive Street. For some reason none of the three joined the Marine society, although their father had been much interested in it, having been secretary, treasurer, and president.

"Capt. Jones was one of the younger ones that I remember. While still a boy he was washed overboard in a gale off the Cape of Good Hope, but was rescued and lived to a good old age.

"Capt. Daniel Knight had retired before I knew him and lived in [sic] the block at the head of Green Street.

"**Capts. Knapp and Kezer were among the later masters.** Capt. Knapp and one of the Bayleys built the last two houses in town that were erected by shipmasters. They are opposite the Mall and Dr. Clancy lived in the lower one of the two. Capt. Kezer, as I told before, saved Capt. Cheever's life when threatened by a mutinous sailor. He had a very long career at sea, and lost his son on one voyage when the boy was washed overboard, in a storm.

"There were three Lunts. Captain Micajah Lunt lived in the house where Col. Barron now resides, for many years. He was for a long time, president of the Merchants National bank, had a counting room -- as it was called -- on Ferry Wharf, and did business as a shipowner. Letters and a journal of his, telling of his being frozen into the James River on a winter voyage, are still in the hands of his grandchildren. His brother George lived at the corner of Parsons and High Streets. In 1843 George Lunt carried food to Liverpool for the distressed Irish, during the famine, and was welcomed with a public reception, at which the generosity of the

American people was praised. Capt. Lunt himself was presented with a fine telescope.

"I recall two Mullikens. Capt. Samuel was lost at sea in my early days. Capt. Moses was in his later years, custodian of the Marine rooms. He, during the Civil War, was one of the Yankee skippers who fell in with the Rebel Raider, 'Alabama'; but, aided by a piece of luck, quick thinking, and a thumping lie, he managed to make his escape. The luck was that the ship's name was almost identical with that of an English ship, which was known to be in those parts, at that time. His son was Professor Samuel Mulliken who was the first student to have the advantage of the Wheelwright Fund.

"**Capt. Moore was the only one of the list that I ever saw set sail from the wharf in a new ship.** I remember his coming down to the wharf in a hack with his daughter, who was afterward Mrs. Stanley, and who was to sail with him. I remember that, as they went up the gangplank, the steward met them and escorted them below. In a very few minutes the captain re-appeared on the quarter-deck in a Scotch cap, having removed the tall silk hat that he had worn, gave the orders for hoisting sail, and the ship left the harbor, never to return to the Merrimac.

"Capt. MacKinney, as the story goes, was picked up, a stray waif on a wharf in Liverpool by one of the Newburyport captains and he remained here. He built and for a number of years lived in the house which I now occupy (227 High Street).[5]

"Capt. Nat Osgood had retired before my memory of him.

"Capt. Pettingell is remembered as driving a pair of horses about the city, but, after his retirement, he seldom got outside of it. He was another of our local skippers who was overhauled by a Confederate raider, but, as his cargo belonged to a neutral nation, he was let off with the payment of a ransom.

"**There were six Pikes:** Edmund, Edmund, Jr., Samuel W., Moses, John, and Bartlett. Edmund, Jr. retired from the sea rather young, went to Philadelphia and engaged in the jewelry business. John Pike was often called Holy Joe, partly because of his dignified appearance and manners. Capt. Samuel was once presented with a fine chronometer by an insurance company for bringing a badly leaking ship safely into port. The widow of Capt. Bartlett Pike built the northern half of the house formerly owned by Mr. Hooper, and there she cared for the children of a merchant whom she had known in Calcutta. Capt. Pike was another whose ship was captured and burned by the 'Alabama.'

"Capt. Page, when at home, always attended church with his mother and made quite an impression on me as he escorted her to her pew. He was the father of ex-mayor Page.

"Of Captains Plummer and Pierce I remember but little.

"**Capt. Raynes built the house at the corner of Bromfield and High streets.** He once rescued 50 persons from a vessel that had been wrecked in a typhoon. They had been four days without food and water.

"Capt. Reed who comes next on my list, was said to have made about one hundred voyages to the West Indies and to have been master of twenty-four ships.

"Capt. Rogers I know little of. He occupied the house, which belonged to Hon. Gayden Morrill.

---

[5] *Southern Essex District Registry of Deeds*: Book 1234:445-446. Henry B. Little, on 15 October 1888, purchased the home of Thomas Mackinney on High Street, near the head of Kent and known as one of the pleasant estates on High Street. The house number at that time was 233, but was changed to 277 High Street. *Southern Essex District Registry of Deeds*: Book 1076:259. Thomas Mackinney purchased the home in 1882 from Charles H. Ireland.

"There were two Simpsons, one who was totally blind for many years, was the father of the late Judge Simpson. He lived on Lime Street. The other, Capt. John Simpson, was caretaker of the Marine Society at one time.

"**Capt. Stone got his master's papers and ship when he was only 21 years of age.** Once, when lying in the harbor at a Porto Rico town, he was boarded by pirates and all his money and clothes were stolen.

"Capt. Stanley was lost at sea and it was believed by some of his friends that disaffection among the crew was the reason. The tale the crew told, however, was that he had been washed overboard.

"There were two Spring captains, father and son; also two Shoofs, father and son. I did not know them well and neither was I acquainted with Capt. Symonds and Capt. Spalding, although the son and daughter of the latter were my schoolmates.

"Capt. Paul Thurlow was a cousin of my father's and was lost in the 'Black Hawk' about 1860. It was the same wreck in which Capt. Cook's son was lost.

"Capt. Wills lived in the house owned by Mr. Trask. He was, I believe, one of six brothers, several of whom had lived in Calcutta as merchants.

"Capt. Woods, the last one on my list, during the Mexican War was in command of a transport, taking troops to the Mexican coast. One of his passengers was Robert E. Lee, then a member of the staff of General Winfield Scott.

"**I find that I have omitted three,** Capt. Varina, who, in retiring from the sea, was a coal-dealer in town; Capt. Charles Smith, who lived in what was called the Stedman house of Federal street, but who left Newburyport when his daughter was married; and a Capt. Pritchard.

These old shipmasters were of a race, which is now extinct, but they made a deep impression on the times in which they lived. With one, or possibly two, exceptions, they were all New England Yankees.

Chapter 9

COMMENTARIES ON HENRY B. LITTLE: 1951 AND 1956

HENRY BAILEY LITTLE STARTS 53RD TERM AS INSTITUTION PRESIDENT[6]

Newburyport Daily News
January 22, 1951

"The grand old man of Newburyport and American Banking, Henry Bailey Little, was re-elected to a 53rd consecutive term as president of the Institution for Savings in Newburyport and Vicinity, at the annual meeting. The meeting was held in the bank yesterday virtually on the eve of Mr. Little's 100th birthday anniversary.

---

[6] *Newburyport Daily News*. The full text of this article can be found in the January 22, 1951 issue. Pg. 85.

"After President Little and the board were re-elected, a birthday luncheon was given in his honor. Mr. Little thanked them and said: 'that when he was elected the first time as successor to Edward S. Moseley, it was by a two-vote margin.'

"Dr. Hurd made the following remarks. 'We are here to celebrate the centenary of the birth of the president of this bank. It is apparent to all of us that he carries his years in a truly remarkable fashion. He presides over our meetings and he comes here daily to consider the business of the bank and to act as consultant in all its transitions.

" 'This in itself is enough to excite wonder, accustomed as we are to regard as generally true the Psalmist's dictum that "The days of our years are three score and 10": but it is not for exceeding the usual span of life in this extraordinary manner that this event is chiefly significant.' "

Bank President 52 Years

"Mr. Little has been president of this bank for 52 years. In this position and throughout his long life he has shown the highest qualities of wisdom, integrity and faithfulness. In all these years there has not been the slightest blemish upon his honor. His ability as a business man has been held in the highest esteem by all who have known him and, above all else, he has been public spirited, gracious and kindly. Therefore, he has won the affection of his fellow citizens as well as that of a multitude, far and near, outside of this city…."

OLDSTERS JOIN VOTING MILLIONS

Boston American, Boston, Massachusetts
November 6, 1956

"Three lively centenarians hustled to the poles in Massachusetts, while scores of voters pushing toward the century mark cast their votes in many voting places across the state. Newburyport's 106 year old retired banker Henry B. Little went early to his voting place, while his townsmen Charles L. Davis, 100, a druggist, walked across the street to vote."

"HEAP OF LIVIN" RECALLED BY 61 CENTENARIANS

Boston Herald, Boston, Massachusetts
December 2, 1956

"Henry B. Little, retired banker who now lives at 37 Devon Rd., in Chestnut Hill, Mass. is 105. He first voted in 1872 for Ulysses S. Grant. One of the first persons to own a telephone in Newburyport. The last to give up his carriage horses."

BANKER IS HONORED 106TH BIRTHDAY

Boston Herald, Boston, Massachusetts
January 5, 1957

"Newburyport: Henry Bailey Little was flooded with good will and congratulations today on his 106th birthday and anniversary. The retired banker, in good health, and jolly spirits gave part of his birthday cake to his relatives who called on him at his home, 227 High Street. As usual he said the recipe for longevity is 'be moderate in all things.' "

Henry Bailey Little at Age 101.
Courtesy of the Museum of Old Newbury.

Chapter 10

OBITUARY AND TRIBUTES TO THE LIFE OF HENRY BAILEY LITTLE

NEWBURYPORT DAILY TIMES

"**1957 August 15. Reported that Henry Bailey Little, 106, born on January 3d, 1851, had died.**"

LAST RITES SUNDAY AT UNITARIAN CHURCH
1957 August 16

"The funeral of Henry Bailey Little will be held Sunday afternoon at 3 at the Church of the First Religious Society (Unitarian).

"Mr. Little died at 10:50 a.m. yesterday at the Anna Jaques hospital where he had been a patient for a month.

"The Rev. Laurence Hayward, minister emeritus of the Unitarian church will officiate at the services.

"Cremation will follow, and the burial of ashes will be at the convenience of the family.

"Those who desire may send a memorial donation to the Anna Jaques Hospital.

"Mr. Little was married to the late Miss Fanny Gray of Newburyport in 1878. The couple had nine children, four of whom survive their parents. They are Leon M. Little, Chestnut Hill; Mrs. Charles D. Baker, Jr., Mrs. Robert M. Driver and Mrs. H. Greenleaf Noyes, all of this city. Other children included Edward H. Little, former school committeeman who died in 1919, Charles Gray Little, one of New England's aviators in World War I, killed in the crash of the Z R 2 [airship] in England in 1921. Three other children, John, Allen and Marion died in childhood.

"Mr. Little leaves, in addition, 14 grandchildren and 30 great-grandchildren."

PASSING OF HENRY BAILEY LITTLE RECALLS SERVICE TO THE COMMUNITY
1957 August 16

"The lengthiest career in the history of this city came to an end yesterday with the passing of Henry Bailey Little.

"It is not enough to note merely that Mr. Little reached a great age, although he would have attained 107 years on next January 3. It is how Mr. Little spent those years that gave him the stature he enjoyed.

"It is significant that Mr. Little will be remembered chiefly by the more recent generations as a banker. Stories which received national attention during recent years made much of the fact that he actively

First Religious Society Unitarian Universalist (Church),
26 Pleasant Street, Newburyport, Massachusetts.
Courtesy of the Museum of Old Newbury, Snow Photograph Collection.

participated in the affairs of the Institution for Savings for more than half a century, the last 25 years of which came at a time when most men had retired. But Mr. Little used his lifetime to even greater service than that given to his banking interests.

"H. B. Little was born Jan. 3, 1851, shortly after Newburyport became a city, and knew all but two of the mayors who have served this community. He could recall memories of the Hon. Caleb Cushing from the time of the latter's return from Spain where he served as Minister. He was present for the inauguration of the Historical Society of Old Newbury as Mr. Cushing's special attendant, and was vice president of it at the time of his death. He attended the Putnam school when there were three high schools in this city. He enjoyed in later life, attending the annual senior prom at Newburyport High school, where he consistently represented 100 percent of the living members of his class.

"Mr. Little could recall watching some 100 shipping vessels under construction in the shipyards of the city, as he could speaking with the great-great-grandson of Nicholas Noyes, the first English settler to step on the shore of Newbury.

"**Mr. Little entered banking as a clerk at the First National bank, but shortly thereafter, took a position with the E. P. Dodge company as bookkeeper.** He was taken into partnership a few years later, and remained in the shoe manufacturing business for 50 years with that company, and later the Ireland Grafton company, from which he retired in November of 1922.

"Active politically, Mr. Little served on the school committee, the old common council, the city council, the board of assessors, and as a commissioner of the sinking fund. He ran for congress from the Sixth district in 1892 and in 1894, and for secretary of state for Massachusetts on the Democratic ticket in 1904.

"Among the numerous offices he held were those of a director of the American Unitarian Association, Treasurer of the First Religious Society of Newburyport, president of the Newburyport Institution for Savings, director of the First and Ocean National bank, of Ipswich of which institution he was the founder and the first president; and treasurer of the Anna Jaques hospital, which institution was of great personal interest to him.

"He was trustee of the Putnam School fund, of the Burley fund for the YMCA, and had been active in the Bethel Society and the Massachusetts Society for the prevention of Cruelty to Animals."

STATEMENTS OF FRIENDS OF HENRY BAILEY LITTLE ON HIS PASSING
1957 August 16

"Several of Henry Bailey Little's business associates commented on his passing today. Among those interviews were:"

Emery Hollerer

"Emery Hollerer, executive vice-president and treasurer of the Institution for Savings who worked beside Mr. Little for many years said that even when the banker had passed his 100th birthday 'he used to come to work, summer or winter, rain or shine, every day.'

"Emery Hollerer felt 'it was a privilege to work beside a man who was considered one of the ablest bankers in the country by both Boston and New York banking circles.'"

Rev. Laurence Hayward

"The Rev. Laurence Haywood [Hayward], pastor emeritus of the First Religious Society, Unitarian, said Mr. Little was a devoted churchman and, 'in fact, one might call him a pillar of the church.'

"As a Unitarian he served three terms as director of the American Unitarian Association, the national body of the Unitarians.

" 'Personally,' the Rev. Haywood [Hayward] said, 'Mr. Little was known as a man of very forceful character, devoted to his convictions in all lines whether they were religious or political or anything else.' "

Willis F. Atkinson

"Willis F. Atkinson, President of the Institution for Savings, and associated for many years with Mr. Little on the board of investment, said he has a great deal of respect for Mr. Little both as a banker and as a man. He considered Mr. Little as a friend and if he had a question 'I would ask him and I would have great respect for his answers as he was human [sic] and considerate.' "

William Balch

"William Balch, who was at the Institution for Savings for 61 years and succeeded Mr. Little as president remembers Mr. Little was there at the bank before him. He remembers Mr. Little was a wonderful man for the bank with an 'extra-fine' judgment on investments. He said in all the years he worked with Mr. Little he found him a very agreeable man to work with and Balch always received Mr. Little's cooperation."

Malcolm G. Ayers

"It was my great privilege to have known Mr. Little for many years. He was a fine gentleman, and a generous public spirited citizen.

While he established an outstanding reputation in business and banking circles, he also left the imprint of his amazing energy and noteworthy integrity in other spheres of community life. He served in various capacities in the City Government and the city is the beneficiary of his unswerving devotion to the public duties which he agreed to perform. On the School Board and in the City Council he was an inspiration to his younger associates who were confident that they were safe in following his leadership. He was fearless in upholding those causes of the soundness of which he had unfailing convictions. It is recalled that in one instance, as a private citizen, he engaged counsel and took successfully to the Supreme Court of the Commonwealth a question involving the important subject of municipal budgetary procedure.

"Outstanding among Mr. Little's social interests was his membership in the Fortnightly Club of which he was one of the founders. The papers which he prepared and read at its meetings teemed with historical data, and reminiscences of events which occurred in his early life.

"Mr. Little gave generously of his time and talent in support of many charitable enterprises. One of his most notable services was that rendered over a long period of time as treasurer of the Anna Jaques Hospital."

Richard F. Churchill

"Richard F. Churchill, president of the First and Ocean National Bank, said that besides the many years Mr. Little had been active in the business and banking life of the community he would be greatly missed for his activity in behalf of the religious and charitable associations of the city. 'In my association with him of over 20 years,' he said, 'he has been a wise councilor and friend.' "

Mayor Henry Graf, Jr.

"The passing of Henry Bailey Little, the city's oldest citizen and the nation's oldest banker, can be considered the closing of an era that spanned two centuries. During his long lifetime, Mr. Little witnessed four wars and tremendous changes in the American way of life. I feel that his death ends the city's link with the historic past. It is difficult to realize that Mr. Little was not only an eye witness but a part of the events recorded in the histories of Newburyport, and that we now consider as having transpired beyond man's memory.

"Henry Bailey Little served his community in many ways, as a banker and as an elected and appointed member of the city government. His actions in these capacities were guided by his many years of understanding and experience, and guided by the wisdom that only the passing of time can bestow upon an individual.

"The many years of life granted Mr. Little were carefully and fully used so that the stewardship of our eldest citizen was for the benefit of the people of Newburyport during this eventful century."

MANY ATTEND RITES FOR LITTLE
6 GRANDSONS ARE PALLBEARERS
August 19, 1957

"With about 200 persons in attendance, funeral services for Henry Bailey Little 'grand old man' of American banking, who died Thursday at 106, were held yesterday afternoon.

"The services were in the Unitarian church, with the Rev. Laurence Hayward, minister emeritus, officiating. Mrs. Edith True Marshall was organist.

"Among those in attendance were persons affiliated with the banking business, societies with which Mr. Little was affiliated and the Anna Jaques Hospital. Representing the city government were Mayor Henry Graf, Jr., and Councilors Arthur J. Smith, George H. Lawler, Jr., and Arthur J. Smith [again]. Municipal flags were flown at half-staff in tribute to Mr. Little.

"The pallbearers were Henry B. Little II, Edmund G., William H. and Leon L. Noyes, Charles D. Baker III and Stephen Little, grandsons of Mr. Little. They also served as ushers.

"The body was taken to Harmony Grove in Salem for cremation. Committal services were arranged for this afternoon at the family lot in Oak Hill Cemetery with the Rev. Mr. Hayward officiating."

Gravestone of Henry and Fanny Little, Oak Hill Cemetery, Newburyport, MA.
Photograph by Skip Motes – March 24, 2019.

AN EDITORIAL: HENRY BAILEY LITTLE
August 19, 1957

"The death of Henry Bailey Little at 106 on August 14 broke the final remaining link with this city's firsthand acquaintance with the historical past. It removed from the scene a man who had much to do with shaping of this city's destiny, as both a business and social influence. What businessman during the past 50 years could have ignored his potential influence in the Newburyport scene, or which working family has not, at one time or another, made reference to 'Henry Bailey Little' when explaining to its members why something was or was not so?

"Mr. Little was a rugged individualist who lived to see the importance of the individual gradually diminished by the rise of the state. His own success as a banker and businessman came during the years of laissez-faire, when a man could pit his skills and courage against those of other men with a minimum of opposition from the government. And yet, Mr. Little reached the top of his society without abusing others along the way.

"In attaining a great age, the while retaining his lively interest in local affairs, Mr. Little became something of a legend. He was probably credited with more things that never happened than any local man in our history. For those who accepted lack of 'progress' with resignation and no imagination, Henry Bailey Little became the symbol of their frustrations. He became synonymous with the 'they' in 'They won't let it happen in Newburyport.' But this very attitude served as a tribute to his stature in the community.

"Mr. Little will be remembered for many things by many people. Those who knew him best will remember him for his deeper qualities, which won him broad respect. For most of us who knew him only from printed and spoken reports of his life in recent years, there remains a picture of a solid citizen who lived out his generous span of years without faltering. He sought responsibilities which lesser men ignored, and accepted gracefully those thrust upon him. On the occasions when the public was able to share his remarks, they found a ready wit, warmly served.

"The numerous stories of Henry Bailey Little are already woven into the fabric of legend. It remains to be seen whether the influence of the legend in the future will be as marked as was the influence of the man during his lifetime."

1957 August 31, *Boston Herald*. Deaths:

"August 15. Newburyport. Mr. Henry Bailey Little, 106, who was thought to be the oldest active banker in the nation at his retirement in 1953."

Addendum I

MR. LITTLE ON THE MAYORS OF NEWBURYPORT

Two loose pages by H. B. Little, Courtesy of the Museum of Old Newbury file: Historical Society Papers K-R.

"I presume that I am probably the only one in Newburyport who remembers all the Mayors and I thought it would be interesting to take this subject for our meeting. The city of Newburyport is not as old as I am but it was born the same year. **The first Mayor, Caleb Cushing,** probably none of you remember. He had a much more varied experience than most men. He was a member of the cabinet of President Pierce; U. S. minister to China; he was the leading council for the United States in prosecuting a case against Great Britain concerned with the damages of the privateer Alabama, which the British Government had been notified to detain in port but failed so to do. I never came in personal contact with him but once, and that was at the time of the organization of the Historical Society of Old Newbury.

This was organized at a large public dinner in a tent erected on Oldtown Green. Cushing was the principal speaker and I was the one who took him to the dinner.

"**Mayors Johnson and Davenport** I did not know. **The fourth Mayor, William Cushing,** was a brother of Caleb. He was interested in shipping; had an office down on one of the wharves.

"**Albert Currier** who followed William Cushing was a contractor and builder; did quite an extensive business.

"**George W. Jackman, Jr.** was a shipbuilder and built two of the largest vessels ever built on the Merrimac. They were the Ontario [and] Erie steamers, but they proved a failure as far as business was concerned. His home on Woodland Street was later owned by Mayor Michael Cashman.

"**Isaac H. Boardman** was interested in shipping and coastal trade and likewise had an office on one of the wharves. His home is now occupied by Dr. R. W. Pearson.

"**Wm. H. Graves** was a retired shipmaster trading with China and the East Indies.

"**Eben F. Stone** was a lawyer who had various offices the last of which was representative in Congress [*sic*] during the Civil War he was a colonel in the 48th Mass. regiment, saw service in Louisiana. His home is the red brick house on State Street, corner Greenleaf.

"**Nathaniel Pierce** was a lawyer but as I have heard the story he had trouble with one of the judges and in my day never practiced in the courts but confined his business with office work.

"**Elbridge G. Kelly** was a dentist by profession, lived in the Dexter house and sometime after middle life it was generally supposed he had trouble with his family and went to London and practiced his profession there where he died.

"**Warren Currier** was a member of the firm, Sumner, Swasey and Currier, who occupied one of the wharves. They did a considerable business with Southern ports and the West Indies.

"**Benjamin F. Atkinson** was the proprietor of the Ocean House and also was a shipbuilder.

"**Jonathan Smith** was the Superintendent of one of the cotton mills. He had no expectation of being elected and ran as a Prohibitionist and was [so] upset by his election that he walked the floor all night.

"**John James Currier** you will all recognize as the author of the History of Newbury and Newburyport. He was the son of a shipbuilder.

"**Benjamin Hale** was admitted to the Bar but I do not remember that he had any regular practice."

Addendum II

NEWBURYPORT AS I KNEW IT

BY H. B. LITTLE

"When the riverside people felt that their interest differed materially from the farming community they petitioned the legislature to be incorporated as a separate town. As originally laid out it commenced at South Street now Bromfield and North now Oakland Street and at the head of these streets the line extended out to the open county until they crossed nearly out to Turkey hill.

"Years ago in travelling across country with my children I came across a boundary stone. In 1851 Belleville and Joppa were added.

"I remember very well when we had five cotton mills -- one a frame building situated just above the bridge across the river. The frame building made a great impression on me as it was the first large building that I ever saw lighted. It was destroyed by fire when I was quite young. The other cotton mills were the Ocean on Monroe street, the James down on Salem street now occupied by a shoe factory, and the Globe which extended from the upper side of Federal street down to Water street. This was taken down. The Bartlett mill at Pleasant and Inn streets was later destroyed by fire and while the fire was raging I spent most of the time on the top of [our] shoe factory looking at the cinders.

"I was a bank clerk at the First National Bank which was down on the lower side of State street nearly down to the Market Square and at this time there was one small shoe factory on Merrimac street and during my banking experience another small one started on the upper floor of a building down near lower State street.

"Later a three-story building on the corner of Hale's court and Pleasant street was occupied by two different firms one of which built the factory on Pleasant street which eventually was continued through to Prince place. Other factories were built later and shoe manufacturing became the principal industry of the town.

"I probably have mentioned the shoe business first because I was an interested party. The real life of the town however was on the river front. I remember four shipyards, three of them at Belleville. These were John Currier's, George W. Jackman's and Currier and Townsend and one below the bridge of whose management I am rather uncertain. The last full rigged ship the 'Mary L. Cushing' was built in 1884 but there were smaller crafts built for years later. The wharves were also busy. It is curious to note that none of the full rigged ships that were built here ever returned although many of them built here returned to Boston. They were largely for the China and Calcutta trade. Among the later ones built three of them were the Importer, Exporter and Reporter all managed by Sumner, Swasey and Currier who occupied the building now used by Swift. In those days before the City Railroad was built the dock came right up to Water street and the traffic on the street went up to the bowsprits.

"When I was quite young during a heavy Northeaster it was reported in the next issue of the paper that of the 102 vessels in port several were damaged and one giving the name sunk in the war [*sic*]. In those days quite a fleet of schooners went to the coast of Labrador fishing for codfish and when received in Newburyport was cured on fish flakes on the lower part of Water street and it covered acres of ground. There was also several vessels fishing for mackerel which were packed on shore and I remember that my Father used to have a keg of same in such sizes as he wanted them for winter use. All the lumber, grain and coal came by water. Robert Bailey [Bayley] and Sons who occupied the building now utilized by Yerxa and Company with wharf adjoining was covered with hogsheads of molasses, which I presume went largely to the Caldwells for the production brewing of rum. I have a carboy of Caldwell's rum now. One of my friends got a hold of a barrel and divided it. I got three carboys.

"D. & I. Hale who owned City Wharf just off the market square had their counting room on the second floor of the building at the end of the wharf. We had counting rooms in those days not offices. The Hales had a fleet of coasters named The Heron, The Huntress, The Hiawatha. I remember only these three. You will note that the names of the vessels all commence with the letter 'H.'

"The business on the river front gradually disappeared the last item being some six or eight years ago with a cargo of lumber delivered by a Nova Scotia vessel. During the time of shipbuilding we also had a number of rope walks. I remember four. These were rough buildings hundreds of feet long. We also had two large hat factories, both of them some distance up Merrimac street. As a help to the shipping were the bakeries of Pearson and butler who furnished crackers and biscuits the latter generally referred to as hard tack and also for general use. My Father always had a barrel of Butler's biscuits for summer use. He used the biscuits for the lunches of the men on the farm. On the long days of summer the men were given hard tack and milk with their lunch.

"What little education I received was graduation [*sic*] from the Putnam Free School, a high school without dead languages. Mine was the last class but one to graduate. It was in some manner consolidated with the Newburyport High School but at the present time the income is used for individual pupils in technical schools.

"William Wheelwright when he wished to give his son a practical education could find no satisfactory place in New England and the boy was sent to Albany. To overcome this deficiency he established a fund the income to be used for the technical education of Newburyport youth. Many have taken advantage of this opportunity for a technical education.

"Many of us feel that we have an excellent hospital that had a small beginning. Anna Jaques was the last of her family of four, a sister and two brothers. None of them ever married. She was considered the invalid of the family and was cared for as such. She outlived them all. Her physician was Dr. Howe and I presume that at some time or other he mentioned the desirability of a hospital. One day when he called she went to her chamber on the second floor and brought down twenty-five thousand dollars in bonds at par value, of which twenty-two thousand were in City of Boston bonds and three thousand dollars in state of Massachusetts bonds. She gave them to Dr. Howe and told him to start a hospital and from that act the hospital was born.

"We formerly had four banks, in one of which I was employed for five years from the time I was sixteen until I was twenty-one. I do not presume that the four banks together did as much business as one of the present banks. Each of the banks had three employees, a cashier, bookkeeper and a boy to run errands. I was the errand boy. Very few persons in my young day[s] kept checking accounts -- now everyone needs one. The deposits of all of the banks were probably half of what each bank has now. Our Institution for Savings is the third one in the State,

Boston and Salem having preceded us. We have deposits from Maine to California and some foreign countries. With reference to shipbuilding it is curious to..." (The last pages of this text are missing.) Courtesy of the Museum of Old Newbury.

Addendum III

OLDEST BANK PRESIDENT, 99 PROUD BOAST OF NEWBURYPORT

BY W. E. PLAYFAIR, *BOSTON HERALD*

October 22, 1950

"NEWBURYPORT, Oct. 21–This little Massachusetts city boasts, among its many other distinctions, the oldest active bank president in the county.

"He is Henry Bailey Little, head of the Institution for Savings, who is only two months short of his 100th birthday, yet goes to his office every day and carries out all the duties of his position.[7, 8]

"Except for impaired hearing and failing eyesight, he might seem to have discovered the secret of the 'fountain of youth,' but if you ask him to explain his remarkable records, he will tell you something like this:

" 'Learn to adjust yourself to change and don't be disturbed too much over things you cannot control.'

ESTABLISHED 1820.

Institution for Savings
in Newburyport and its vicinity.

BANKING HOUSE, No. 93 STATE STREET,

Dividends payable on the Fourth Wednesday of April and October.
OPEN DAILY 8.30 TO 2.

CONDITION OF THE INSTITUTION APRIL 27, 1909.

Liabilities.		Resources.	
Deposits	$7,004,554.89	Public Funds	$2,026,500.00
Guaranty Fund	345,000.00	City and Town Notes	84,800.00
Profits	225,020.24	Bank Stock	253,920.00
		Railroad Bonds	2,052,000.00
		Loans on Real Estate	1,638,910.20
		Loans on Personal Securities	1,136,291.78
		Loans on Bank Stock	1,855.00
		Banking House	25,000.00
		Real Estate by Forclosure	43,079.10
		Real Estate in Possession	448.55
		Securities taken for Debts	96,502.16
		Cash in Banks on Interest	213,656.23
		Cash on Hand	1,612.11
$7,574,575.13		$7,574,575.13	

The Front and Back Sides of an Institution for Savings Card, 1909. Courtesy of the Museum of Old Newbury.

President.
HENRY B. LITTLE.

Vice Presidents.
L. B. CUSHING,   GILMAN W. BROWN,   T. C. SIMPSON.

Trustees.

L. B. Cushing,	Charles W. Moseley,	Henry B. Little,
Thomas C. Simpson,	Paul A. Merrill,	H. R. Perkins,
L. D. Cole,	Edward F. Little,	N. N. Jones,
Geo. W. Piper,	Frank O. Woods,	Gilman W. Brown,
James C. Colman,	W. Burke Little,	Davis F. Noyes,
Frank F. Morrill,	Daniel N. Little,	J. H. Ireland,
Robert E. Burke,	John E. McCusker,	John H. Wheeler,
L. N. Kent,	G. A. Philbrick.	

William Balch, Treasurer.   Myron R. Currier, Bookkeeper.
George F. Avery, Secretary.   Hallett W. Noyes, Bookkeeper.

Russell E. Briggs, Auditor.

"Change! He has seen plenty of it. 'It's a new world altogether,' as he puts it, since he was born Jan. 3, 1851, in neighboring Newbury. At that time none of the facilities deemed necessary for living today were available except the railroads and the telegraph.

"How do you keep young? One way is by meeting progress halfway, and Henry B. Little, a true modern in spite of his birthdate, has done just that. His was the third home in the city to have a telephone. He had one of the very first oil furnaces, one of the first electric refrigerators, one of the first electric razors.

"He was a little slow in welcoming the gasoline era, but that was because he loved horses. He was the last person in Newburyport to give up, keeping his horses until 1920. But when he went into automobiles he did it with a will, though he never learned to drive himself. But he added to his fondness of long ocean voyages a yen for long motor jaunts.

"To this day he will not listen to the radio and he has no television set. But this is merely because he lets nothing interfere with his reading. His favorite literature is history and biography and he has developed an extraordinary knowledge of American political history.

"Members of his family will tell you that Little has kept himself young by his ability to substitute younger generations for his companions as his contemporaries died off.

---

[7] *Boston Herald*, Boston, Massachusetts, pg. 14. Photograph. " 'The Hardest Years Behind Him' Henry B. Little who will be 100 tomorrow, was sworn in yesterday for his 52d term as president of the Institution for Savings in Newburyport. Secretary Hallet W. Noyes administers oath." January 2, 1951.

[8] The News of Henry B. Little's 100th birthday, and the oldest banker appeared in newspapers in fourteen states: CA, CT, GA, IL, ID, KY, LA, MA, MI, NB, NC, OH, RI, WA.

" 'He was pleased with his children' says his son Leon M. Little, vice-president of the New England Trust Company, Boston, 'delighted about his grandchildren and most enthusiastic about his great grandchildren. Three and four-year-olds take to him naturally and it is amusing to hear them shouting at him in their high little voices trying to make him hear.' "

Attended a Rural School

"Born on a Newbury farm, he attended a rural school in that town and the Putnam Free School in Newburyport, one of the few high schools of the day. He planned to be a civil engineer, and he would have been one of the early students at MIT if that plan had carried through.

"But to earn money for his courses, Little got a job as messenger at the First National Bank, now the First and Ocean, and that settled his career. He liked banking.

" 'That's changed, too,' he says wryly. 'In my early days only a few people kept checking accounts. Now everybody does. And we didn't know much about investments then, just railroads and a few manufacturing establishments. Now everything is done by corporations.'

"From the bank he went with E. P. Dodge, who started a successful shoe business in Newburyport. Later they sold out and Little and two others continued to operate another shoe concern, the Ireland-Grafton Company, which they had started earlier in Dover, N. H. When he had been in the shoe business 50 years, Little resigned to devote himself to banking. "

Started Ipswich Bank

"In 1899 he became president of the Institution for Savings, third oldest savings bank in the state, which has just declared its 254th consecutive semi-annual dividend. Oldest is the Provident of Boston, and second oldest, the Salem Savings Bank.

"In 1894, with Dodge, he started the First National Bank in Ipswich,[9] and was president of that bank until 1901, when as he tells it, he was 'legislated out of office.' In that year the Legislature passed a law which prevented the same man from being president of a savings bank and a national bank.

"But Little remained a director and, except for a very brief period, the presidency has stayed in the family. One son, the late Edward H. Little, was the bank's head for a time, and the current president is Leon M. Little.

"Last month the father broke ground for a new building for the Ipswich bank, the third it [sic] in existence.

"This near-centenarian lives in the future, rather than in the past, but his remembrance of things past is phenomenal. Some years ago the Rockefeller Foundation chose Newburyport as the type of city for a study of the old American stock. Little was able to tell the researchers–from memory–the names and stories of everybody who had built and lived in every house on High street from Newbury line to Three Roads, a distance of four miles. "

---

[9] *Boston Herald*, Boston, Massachusetts. " 'Bank's Founder, 99, Starts New Building.' Ninety-nine-year-old Henry B. Little of Newburyport, who founded the First National Bank of Ipswich in 1892 with $1000, broke ground for the bank's $125,000 new building on Market street today. He was the bank's first president and still serves on the board of directors." H. B. Little was one of the eleven organizers of the bank." September 7, 1950.

Served on Boards

"He has served his part in public affairs, having been treasurer of the Anna Jaques Hospital since 1902, served on the school board and water board, and as a member of the city council for eight years. He was over 70 the last time he ran for the council.

" 'It was up to somebody to do something about it,' he explains.

"So he found himself a city councilor under Mayor 'Bossy' Gillis, and the two, unexpectedly enough, go along very well. 'Bossy' had respect for the banker's age and ability.

"In politics he had always been extremely active. He describes himself as 'a longlife free trader and hard money man, and sometimes Republican.' "

Bryan Gold Democrat

"He supported Cleveland, thought Rutherford Hayes never got fair credit for 'his remarkable clean-up job after Grant,' and was a Gold Democrat at the time of Bryan. He attended the convention that nominated Palmer and Buckner for the third party in the McKinley-Bryan fight.

"He is particularly proud of the fact that he has 35 living descendants, his son Leon, three daughters, Mrs. Charles D. Baker, Mrs. Robert M. Driver and Mrs. H. Greenleaf Noyes, all of this city; 14 grandchildren; and 17 great grandchildren.

"His meetings from time to time with family groups in his colonial home on High street, he says, are far more important than remembering the Battle of Bull Run–which he does, quite clearly."

Addendum IV
WALDO PEIRCE, ARTIST
1884-1970

"A Painter never retires until he can't lift a brush." Waldo[1]

Cover portrait: *Portrait of Henry B. Little, with Studies of Hands.* Watercolor and pencil. It was signed January 14, 1952, by the artist and inscribed, "To Mrs. [Nancy] Noyes and Best wishes, Waldo Peirce." Mrs. Noyes was the wife of H. Greenleaf Noyes, daughter of Mr. H. B. Little.

Waldo Peirce was born in Bangor, Maine, in 1884, son of Mellen Peirce and Anna (Hayford) Peirce. Waldo died in 1970 at Anna Jaques Hospital in Newburyport, Massachusetts. He attended Andover Academy in Andover, Massachusetts, Class of 1903. As a student at Harvard University, Cambridge, Massachusetts, Waldo was initially a member of the Class of '07, but completed his degree in 1908.

Known as a modernist and impressionist, his work was exhibited with Edward Hopper and other major artists in New York City in 1915. During the 1920's he went to Paris, France, and Spain to study art and was a close friend and traveling companion of Ernest Hemingway. He had long been known as a rebel against conventionalism.

He studied at Art Students League in New York City and at the Julian Academy in Paris and traveled widely throughout Europe. He was inspired by French Impressionists and influenced by the Spanish artist.

He had a commission to paint two murals for the post office in Troy, New York, as part of the Treasury Section of Painting and Sculpture in 1938. The Section was a program to assist artists after the depression era in the 1930s.

Peirce received an honorary degree from Colby College, Waterville, Maine in 1957.[2] He purchased his home at 43 Market Street, Newburyport, Massachusetts in 1961,[3] where he had a studio and also an art studio located at No. 1 Threadneedle Alley, off State Street. He was a very familiar person to see in town, being a quite large and robust man, and was known to always have a pipe in his mouth. He was often seen at the Grog (then Leary's Lunch & The Pilot House), and at Fowles on State Street, both close to his studio. He spent summers in Searsport, Maine.

He was a member of the Newburyport Art Association in 1952, and while not very active, did participate occasionally.

Peirce was known to be a prolific painter, and his works are held in American and European art museum collections. His papers are in the collection of the Library of Congress, Washington, D.C. and Colby College, Waterville, Maine.

---

[1] Witteveld, Chris, "Waldo Peirce, the Man and the Artist in Newburyport." *Newburyport Daily News*. September 16, 1972.

[2] https://www.colby.edu/specialcollections/about/waldo-peirce/.

[3] *Southern Essex District Registry of Deeds*: Book 4857:329.

Photograph of Waldo Peirce in 1960, by Michael Peirce.
Used with permission of Michael Peirce.

More information on Waldo Peirce can be read in two articles published in the North Shore section of the *Newburyport Daily News* (preserved in Newburyport Public Library's Archival Center). These are "Waldo Peirce, the Man and the Artist, in Newburyport," by Chris Witteveld, printed September 16, 1972, and "Waldo Peirce a Portrait of an Artist by Two Friends," written by Francis W. Hatch and Truman Nelson, March 28, 1970. Colby College also has an article on Waldo Peirce on its website in "Special Collections" at https://www.colby.edu/specialcollections/about/waldo-peirce/.

INDEX

A
Albany, NY, 80
Algeria, 4
American Banknote Co., 40
Amesbury, 41
Andrews, John A.
    governor, 10
Arizona, 42
arms making, 32
artillery company, 13
Atkinson, Benjamin F.
    mayor, 75
    proprietor, Ocean House, 75
    ship builder, 75
Atkinson, Willis F., 66
    president, Institution for Savings, 66
automobiles, 13, 85
Ayers, Malcolm G., 66
Azores, 4

B
Bailey Hat Co., 39
Baileys, 12
Baker, Charles D., III
    grandson of H. B. Little, 69
Baker, Charles D., Jr., Mrs.
    daughter of H. B. Little, 7, 9, 62, 88
Baker, John I., 10
bakery, 11
    Butler's, 79
    Pearson, 79
Balch, Capt., 46
Balch, William, 66
    president, Institution for Savings, 66
banks
    First and Ocean, 86
    First and Ocean National Bank, 1
    First and Ocean National Bank in Newburyport, 1
    First and Ocean National Bank, of Ipswich, 65
    First National Bank, 28
    First National Bank of Ipswich, 1
    Institution for Savings, 5fn, 29, 29fn, 30, 80, 84, 86
    Mechanics National Bank, 36, 41
    Merchant's Bank, 29
    Merchants National Bank, 50
    New England Trust Co., 86
    Ocean Bank, 28fn, 36
    Ocean National Bank, 37, 38
    Provident of Boston, 87
    Salem Savings Bank, 87
Bannister, William B., 31
Barron, Col., 50
Bartlett, Capt., 10
Bayleys, 45, 50
Belleville, 77
    church, 37
    shipyards, 78
Bethel Society, 65
Boardman, Isaac H., 74
    coastal trade, 74
    mayor, 74
Bogardus, Capt., 46
bonds
    City of Boston, 80
    State of MA, 80
Boston, 5fn, 18, 22, 29, 36, 42, 65, 78, 81
Boston theatre, 42
Bray, Isaac, Capt., 46
Brays, 46
British Government, 73
Brooks, Capt., 46
Brown, John
    hanging of, 10
Brown, Laurence, Capt., 45

Brown, Nicholas, Capt., 45
Bryan, 88
Burnhome estate, 36
Burrill, Capt., 13
Butler's biscuits, 21, 79

C

Calcutta, 45, 52, 53
Caldwell Rum, 18, 79
California
    bank deposits, 81
    gold excitement, 37
    postage, 12
    Senator Sargent, 39
candles, 11
Cape of Good Hope, 50
cargos, 11, 21, 51, 79
carriage horses, 57
Cashman, Michael, Mayor, 74
central heating, 11
Charlestown, MA, 42
Chattanooga, TN, 41
Cheever, Capt., 47, 50
Chestnut Hill, MA, 57
China, 18, 73, 74, 78
Churches
    American Unitarian
        Association, 4, 65, 66
    Belleville, 37
    First Religious Society
        Unitarian
        Universalist, 63, 66
Churchill, Richard F.
    president, First and
        Ocean National
        Bank, 67
City Railroad, 18, 25, 78
Civil War, 10, 11, 13, 22, 36, 46, 51, 74
    Confederate raider, 51
    southern sympathies, 46
Clancy, Dr., 50
Clarkson, 45

Cleveland, President, 41, 88
coal dealer, 53
cod, 18, 21, 79
coffee, 46
Coffin, Amos
    director, First National
        Bank, 28
Coffin, Charles H., 36
    dry goods store, 36
    first president, First
        National Bank, 28, 37
Colonial Manor, The, 42
comb shops, 32
commercial banks, 29
Cook, Henry, Capt., 46, 53
    director, First National
        Bank, 28, 46
Cook, Mrs.
    son's death, 47
coppery, 38
cordage, 20
cotton, 45
cotton yarns, 31
Couch, Capt., 46
    governor's council, 46
    mayor, 46
    school committee, 46
Couch, Robert
    director, First National
        Bank, 28
crackers and biscuits
    hard-tack, 79
Cross, Henry M., 41
    Gamewell Fire Alarm
        Co., 41
    Civil War prisoner, 41
Cunard Steamship Co., 37
Currier, Albert
    contractor and builder, 74
    mayor, 74
Currier, John, Jr., 39
Currier, John James, 39, 75
    author of History of

        Newbury, Mass. and
        History of Newbury-
        port, Mass., 39, 75
    mayor, 75
Currier, Judge, 13
Currier, Robert, 33
Currier, Warren, Mayor, 75
    Sumner, Swasey and
        Currier, 37, 75
Curtis, Frank, 13
Cushing, Caleb, Hon., 36, 39, 73, 74
    first mayor,
        Newburyport, 73
    member, cabinet of
        President Pierce, 73
    U.S. Minister to China, 73
    U.S. Minister to Spain, 64
Cushing, Sarah M.
    daughter of William
        Cushing, 40
    wife of Robert Toppan, 40
Cushing, William, 36, 40, 74
    fourth mayor,
        Newburyport, 74
    president, Ocean Bank, 36
Custom House Maritime
    Museum, 44
customs receipts, 22
Cutting, Charles H., 42
    president, Anna
        Jaques Hospital, 42

D

Dalton Club, 31
Dame, Luther, 41
    Civil War, 11th
        Massachusetts
        Regiment, 41
    instructor, Putnam Free
        School, 41
Davenport, Mayor, 74
Davis, Charles L.
    druggist, 57

voting at age 100, 57
Dexter house, 74
Dimmick, Dr.
    dentist, 13
Dodge Brothers Shoe Co., 34
Dodge, Chauncey W., 41
    son of John L. Dodge, 41
Dodge, E. P., 40
    brother of John L. Dodge, 41
    shoe business, 3, 41, 86
Dodge, Elisha P., 40
    E. P. Dodge Mfg. Co., 3
    mayor, Newburyport, 41
    member, school board, 41
    president, Mechanics National Bank, 41
    shoe manufacturer, 40
Dodge factory, 31
Dodge, Harry D.
    son of John L. Dodge, 41
Dodge, John L., 41
Dover, NH, 86
dress, boys, 12
    beards, 12
    coat, long-tailed, 12
    coat, Prince Albert, 12
    dundrearies (side whiskers), 12
    hats, flat derby, 12
    hats, tall silk, 12
    hats, wide-brimmed, straw, 12
    mustaches, 12
dress, girls, 12
    dresses, short, 12
    handkerchiefs, 12
    hats or bonnets, 12
    skirts, long, 12
    veils, long, 12
Driver, Josephine M., Mrs.
    daughter of H. B. Little, 7
Driver, Robert M., Mrs.
    daughter of H. B. Little, 9, 62, 88

E

East Indies, 45
Egypt, 4
Eighth Regiment, 13
electric razors, 85
electric refrigerators, 85
Elliott, Capt., 47
Emerton, Capt., 47
England, 40, 45, 62
    Canterbury, 40
E. P. Dodge Mfg. Co., 3, 64
Erie Canal, 41
Europe, 40, 90
Evans, Capt., 47

F

farm provisions, 11
farm wages, 11
farming community, 77
fire engine companies, 13
    hand tubs, 13
First Brigade of MA militia, 13
fish flake, 21
Fiske, Daniel T., Rev., 37
    pastor, Belleville (Congregational) Church, 37
    trustee, Andover Theological Seminary, 37
foreign trade, 43, 44
Fortnightly Club, 7, 67
Fowles, 90
furnace, 85

G

Garrison House, 9
    Spencer-Pierce House, 9
gas plant, 11
gasoline era, 85
Gillis, Bossy, Mayor, 88
government bonds, 46
Governor's Council, 10, 46
Graf, Henry, Jr., Mayor, vii, 68, 69
Grant, Ulysses S., 57
Graves, Alexander, Capt., 47
Graves, Edward, Capt., 47
Graves, William, Capt., 47
    treasurer, Bartlet Mills, 47
Graves, Wm. H., Mayor, 74
Gray, Fanny
    marriage to H. B. Little, 1
Great Britain, 73
Greece, 4
groceries, 11, 35
grocers/grocery stores, 32
    Yerxa and Co., 18, 19, 79

H

hack, 10, 51
Hale, 79
Hale, Benjamin
    admitted to the Bar, 75
    mayor, 75
Hale, Capt., 49
Hale, David and Issac, 18
    D. & I. Hale, 79
Hale, Eliphalet, 49
Hale, George W., 49
Hale, Joshua, 49
Hale, Josiah, 49
Hales, 18, 49, 79
Harris Street Livery Stable, 13
hat factories, 79
Hatch, Francis W.
    friend of Waldo Peirce, 91
Hayward/Haywood, Laurence, Rev., 61, 66, 68, 69
heat, central, 11

Hemingway, Ernest
    friend of Waldo Peirce, 90
Hills, Laura, Miss
    artist, 37, 38
    daughter of Philip K.
        Hills, 37
Hills, Philip K., 37
    city government, 37
    clerk, Ocean National
        Bank, 37
    school board, 37
    secretary and treasurer,
        Institution for
        Savings, 37
Historical Society of Old
    Newbury, 4, 44, 45,
    64, 73, 101
    Changed name to
        Museum of Old
        Newbury, 4, 45, 101
Hollerer, Emery, 65
    treasurer and vice-
        president,
        Institution for
        Savings, 65
Hooper, Mr., 52
Hopper, Edward
    artist, 89
horse and buggy, 12
hospital, 46
    Anna Jaques Hospital, 4,
    5, 39, 40, 42, 61, 62,
    65, 67, 69, 80, 88, 89
hotel
    Ocean House, 75
Howard, Capt., 49
Howe, Francis A., Dr., 39, 40
    founder and president,
        Anna Jaques
        Hospital, 39, 80
    Anna Jaques' physician,
        39, 80
Hoyt, Capt., 49
Hurd, Dr., 56
Huse, Mr., 39

I

importing business, 45
Indian Ocean, 45, 47
Ipswich, MA, 41
Ireland, Charles H., house, 52fn
Ireland-Grafton Co.
    shoe business, 64, 86
Irish famine, 50
Italy, 4

J

Jackman, George W., Jr., 74
    mayor, 74
    shipbuilder, 74
    shipyard, 78
James River, 50
Jaques, Anna, 80
    donated $25,000 to build
        Anna Jaques
        Hospital, 39, 40, 80
Johnson, Frances, Miss, 50
Johnson, Mayor, 74
Johnson, Richard, 50
Johnsons, 50
Jones, Capt., 50
Jones, Oliver, Capt., 21
Joppa, 27, 77

K

Kansas, 41
Kelly, Dr., 12
Kelly, Elbridge G., Dr., 12, 74
    dentist, 74
    mayor, 74
Kelly Field
    Massachusetts militia
        camp, 13
kerosene lamps, 11
Kezer, Fred, Capt., 47, 50
Kinsman, William, 49
Knapp, Capt., 50
Knight, Daniel, Capt., 50

L

laborers, 11
Labrador Coast, 21
Lamson Store Service Corp., 42
Lascar, 47
Lawler, George H., Jr.,
    councilor, 69
Learned, Lorna, Miss, 37
Le Breton, Peter, Capt., 46
Lee, Robert E.
    staff member, General
        W. Scott, 53
Lincoln, President
    assassination, 10
    Wide Awakes' torch
        light parade, 10
Lisbon, 4
Little, Agnes
    niece of H. B. Little, 1, 5fn
Little, Allen
    son of H. B. Little, 62
Little, Amelia
    niece of H. B. Little, 1, 5fn
Little, Catherine, A. (Adams)
    mother of H. B. Little, 1
Little, Charles Gray
    son of H. B. Little, 62
    WWI aviator, killed in
        ZR-2 airship crash
        in England, 1921, 62
Little, Edmund G.
    grandson of H. B. Little, 69
Little, Edward H.
    son of H. B. Little, 62, 87
Little, Edward Henry
    father of H. B. Little, 1,
        14fn
Little, Fanny (Gray)
    death and burial, 5, 69
    mother of 9 children, 1
    wife of H. B. Little, 1, 4, 62
Little, Henry B.
    grandson of H. B. Little, 69

Little, Henry Bailey
- 100th birthday, 55, 65, 83, 85fn
- 101st birthday, 59
- 106th birthday, 58
- Anna Jaques Hospital, 69
  - treasurer of, 4, 65, 67, 88
  - president of, 4
- articles, 9
- associations, 67
- bank clerk, First National Bank, 1, 64, 78
- bank director, First and Ocean National Bank in Newburyport, 4, 28fn
- bank director, First and Ocean National Bank of Ipswich, 65
- bank director, First National Bank, 28fn
- bank director, First National Bank of Ipswich, 1, 4, 28
- bank founder, First and Ocean National Bank of Ipswich, 65
- bank founder, First National Bank of Ipswich, 4, 87, 87fn
- bank messenger, First National Bank, 27, 86
- bank president, 56
- bank president, First and Ocean National Bank of Ipswich, 65
- bank president, First National Bank of Ipswich, 4, 87, 87fn
- bank president, Institution for Savings, 3, 4, 5fn, 28fn, 55, 64, 65, 83,

85fn, 86
- banker-historian, 17, 27, 35, 43
- birth, 1, 9, 61, 64, 73, 85, 86
- bookkeeper, 64
- carriage horses, 57
- city council, 4, 64, 88
- city's oldest citizen, vii, 68
- commissioner, Sinking Fund, 4, 64
- commentaries on, 55
- death, vii, 5, 9, 17, 27, 35, 43, 61, 64, 68, 70, 71
- director, American Unitarian Association, 4, 65, 66
- E. P. Dodge Mfg. Co., 3
- editorial on, 70
- education, 13, 64, 80, 86
- errand boy, 80
- farm life, 11
- father, 1, 9, 10, 11, 21, 46, 53, 79
- founder, First and Ocean National Bank of Ipswich, 4
- funeral at the First Religious Society Unitarian church, 61, 68
- grand old man of banking, 55, 68
- grandchildren, 62, 86, 88
- grandsons, 68, 69
- grave, 69
- great-grandchildren, 62, 86, 88
- hard money man, 88
- home at 227 High Street, 58
- longlife free trader, 88
- marriage, 1
- member, Board of Assessors, 4, 64
- member, City Council, 4,

64, 88
- member, Fortnightly Club, 7, 67
- member, Old Common Council, 4, 64
- member, Newburyport School Committee, 4, 64
- obituary, 61
- oldest bank president, 5, 83
- pallbearers, 68, 69
- papers of, 7, 17, 27, 35, 43, 73
- parents, 1
- passport application, 4
- portrait of, 3
- president, Historical Society of Old Newbury, 4
- president, Society for the Prevention of Cruelty to Animals 4
- retired banker, 57, 58
- ran for Congress Sixth district, 1892, 4, 64
- school life, 12, 13
- school reunion, 14
- telephone, 12, 29, 57, 85
- travels abroad
  - grand tour, 4
- treasurer, First Religious Society, 4, 65
- tributes to, 61, 69, 70, 83
- voting at age 106, 57

Little, John
- son of H. B. Little, 62

Little, Leon M.
- son of H. B. Little, 62, 86, 88
- president, First National Bank in Ipswich, 87
- president, New England

Trust Company, 86
Little, Marion
    daughter of H. B. Little, 62
Little, Stephen
    grandson of H. B. Little, 69
Liverpool, 46, 47, 50, 51
London, 74
Louisiana, 74
lumberjacks, 42
Lunt, George, 50
    Irish famine, 50
Lunt, Micajah, Capt., 50
    president, Merchants National Bank, 50
Lunts, 50
Lynnfield, MA, 10

M

machine shops, 32
mackerel, 11, 18, 21, 79
MacKinney, Capt., 51
MacKinney, Thomas
    home of, 52fn
Madeira, 4
Maine
    Castine, 45
    bank deposits, 81
marine rooms, 51
Marine Society, 44, 50
Market Square, 18, 27, 78, 79
Marshall, Edith True, Mrs.
    organist, 68
Marston, George W., Mrs.
    author of *A California Family*, 46
McCusker, Johnny, Capt., 13
McKinley, President, 88
Meinerth, Carl, 24
Merrimac River, 51, 74
Mexican War, 53
mills, 31
    Bartlet Mill, 31, 47, 78
    cotton mills, 17, 31, 77
    Essex Cotton Mill, 31
    Globe (Steam Mills), 31, 33, 77
    James (Steam Mill), 31, 77
    Ocean (Mill), 31, 77
    yarn mill, 31
Minneapolis, MN, 42
Missouri, 38
Mobile, AL, 42
molasses, 11, 18, 24, 25, 46, 79
Moody, Joseph E., 42
    cabinet maker, 42
    Civil War lieutenant, 42
    Confederate prisoner, 42
Moore, Capt., 51
Morocco, 4
Morrill, Frank F., 41
Morrill, Gayden, Hon., 52
Moseley, Edward Strong, 36
    president, Institution for Savings, 4, 36, 56
    president, Mechanics National Bank, 36
Museum of Old Newbury, 4, 45, 101
    collections, 7, 44
    courtesy of, 14, 15, 20, 24, 25, 29fn, 30, 34, 59, 63, 73, 81, 84

N

Nelson, Jeremiah
    treasurer, Institution for Savings, 29
newpapers
    Boston American, 57
    Boston Herald, 57, 58, 71, 83, 85fn, 87fn
New England Yankees, 54
New York, 22, 37, 49, 65
New York Railroad, 41
Newbury, 1, 9, 20, 64, 85, 86
Newbury line, 27, 87
Newburyport industries
    arms making, 32
    bakeries, 21, 79
    cabinetmaker, 42
    comb shops, 32
    cotton mills, 17, 31, 33, 47, 77
    farming, 1, 11, 21, 79
    fishing, 18, 21, 42, 79
    grocers, 11, 18, 19, 32, 35, 79
    hat brush making, 32
    hat factories, 79
    machine shops, 32
    paper collar making, 32
    rigging, 21, 22, 23
    rope makers, 20, 79
    rum, 18, 79
    shipbuilding, 18, 21, 22, 27, 39, 43, 74, 75, 78
    shipping, 17, 18, 21, 22, 35, 36, 37, 50, 51, 52, 53, 64, 74, 79
    shipyards, 17, 20, 27, 64, 78
    shoe manufacturing, 31, 40, 41, 64, 78
    silverware, 31
    trade, 18, 21, 42, 43, 44, 45, 74, 78
    trolley cars, 32
    wharves, 11, 17, 18, 21, 74, 75, 78
northeaster, 78
Nova Scotia vessel, 21, 79
Noyes, Amos, 38, 39
    first U.S. Assessor under the Internal Revenue Act of Civil War days, 39
Noyes, Edmund G.
    grandson of H. B. Little, 69
Noyes, H. Greenleaf, Mr., 89
Noyes, H. Greenleaf, Mrs., Nancy, daughter of H. B. Little, 62, 88, 89
Noyes, Hallet W., 85fn
Noyes, Leon L.

grandson of H. B. Little, 69
Noyes, Nicholas
    a first settler of Newbury, MA, 1, 64
    great-great-grandfather of H. B. Little, 1, 64
Noyes, William H.
    grandson of H. B. Little, 69

O

Oak Hill Cemetery, 5, 5fn, 69
Ocean House, 75
ocean voyages, 85
Old Common Council, 4, 64
Oldtown, 13
Oldtown Green, 74
Oldtown Hill, 13
Osgood, Nat, Capt., 51

P

Pacific Coast, 36
Page, Capt., 52
    father of Mayor Page, 52
Page, Mayor, 52
paper collar making, 32
Paris Commune, 40
Paris, France, 4, 40
Parton, James, 40
Pearson Bakery, 21, 79
Pearson, R. W., Dr., 74
Peirce, Anna (Hayford)
    Waldo Peirce's mother, 89
Peirce, Mellen, 89
    Waldo Peirce's father, 89
Peirce, Waldo
    Andover Academy, 89
    Art Students League, 90
    artist, 89, 90, 90fn, 91
    Bangor, Maine, 89
    Colby College, 90, 91
    The Grog, 90
    Harvard University, 89
    Hatch, Francis W.

    friend of Waldo, 91
    honorary degree, 90
    Julian Academy in Paris, 90
    Leary's Lunch & The Pilot House, 90
    Library of Congress Waldo's papers, 90
    Nelson, Truman friend of Waldo, 91
    New York City, 89, 90
    Newburyport Art Association, 90
    Paris, France, 89, 90
    Searsport, Maine, 90
    Spain, 89
    Waterville, Maine, 90
Perkins, Major, 47
Petersburg, VA, 42
Pettingell, Capt., 51
Pettingell, John, family, 14fn
Philadelphia, PA, 46, 52
Philadelphia and Reading Coal Co., 41
Pierce, Capt., 52
Pierce, Nathaniel, Mayor, 74
Pierce, President, 73
Pike, Bartlett, Capt., 52
Pike, Bartlett, Capt., widow, 52
Pike, Edmund, 52
Pike, Edmund, Jr., 52
Pike, John, 52
Pike, Moses, 52
Pike, Samuel W., Capt., 52
Plum Island Life-Saving Station, 47
Plummer, Capt., 52
political parties, 88
    Democratic, 4, 64, 88
    Gold Democrat, 88
    Republican, 88
Pope Pius the Ninth, 40
Porto Rico harbor, 53
Portugal, 4

Presidential Election, 1860, 10
Pritchard rigging gang, 21, 23
Pritchard, Capt., 53
Pritchard Co., 23
Putnam Fund, 14

R

railroads, 85, 86
    City Railroad, 18, 25, 78
    New York, 41
    Western, 42
Rand, Edward S., 31
Raynes, Capt., 52
Reed, Capt., 52
Reed, Selwyn, 23
registered vessels, 22
Remick, Timothy
    director, First National Bank, 28
Richardson, Mr.
    home of, 42
Richmond, VA, 10
riggers/rigging gang, 21, 22, 23
riverside people, 77
Robert Bailey (Bayley) and Sons, 18, 18fn, 79
Rockefeller Foundation, 87
Rogers, Capt., 52
rope makers, 20
ropewalks, 79
    Bromfield St., 21
    Chestnut St., 21
    Jackman, 20
    Marlborough St., 21
Russia, 46

S

sailors, 21, 43, 46, 47, 50
salaries, 21
San Diego, 46
San Francisco, 12, 37, 42, 46, 50
Sargent, Senator of California, 39

schools
- Andover Academy, 89
- Andover Theological Seminary, 37
- Boston Latin High School, 42
- Colby College, 90, 91
- Harvard University, 89
- Julian Academy in Paris, 90
- MIT (Massachusetts Institute of Technology), 86
- Newburyport High School, 13, 14, 64, 80
- Putnam Free School, 13, 14, 15, 41, 80, 86
- reunion, 14

schooners, 22
- Labrador fishing fleet, 21, 79

Scott, Winfield, General, 53

Shaw, Edward P.
- director, First National Bank, 28

shipbuilding, 18, 21, 22, 27, 39, 43, 74, 75, 78

shipmasters, 22, 43, 45, 50, 54, 74

shipping, 17, 18, 21, 22, 35, 36, 37, 50, 51, 52, 53, 64, 74, 79

ships
- brig *Tula*, 25
- coaster *Halo*, 18
- coaster *Heron*, 18, 79
- coaster *Hiawatha*, 18, 79
- coaster *Huntress*, 18, 79
- coasters, 11, 18, 79
- last square rigger, 17
- privateer *Alabama*, 45, 73
- rebel raider, *Alabama*, 51, 52
- ship *Black Hawk*, 46, 53

ship *Bengal*, 46
ship *Daniel I. Tenney*, 23
ship *Exporter*, 18, 78
ship *Importer*, 18, 78
ship *J. P. Whitney*, 45
ship *Mary L. Cushing*, 78
ship *Reporter*, 18, 78
schooner *Edward Lemeyer*, 24, 25
steamer *Erie*, 74
steamer *Ontario*, 74

shipyards, 17, 20
- Currier and Townsend, 78
- Currier's, John, 78
- Jackman's, George W., 78

shoe firm/factory/company, 3, 31, 34, 77, 78, 86

Shoofs, 53

sidewalk
- first brick sidewalk, 37

silver trumpet, 13
silverware manufacturing, 31
Simpson, John, Capt., 45
- caretaker, Marine Society, 53
Simpson, Judge, 53
sleeping rooms, 11
Smith, Arthur J., 69
Smith, Charles, Capt., 53
Smith, Jonathan, Mayor
- superintendent, cotton mills, 75

societies
- Bethel Society, 65
- Society for the Prevention of Cruelty to Animals, 4, 65
- Society for the Preservation of New England Antiquities, 1, 5fn

Spain, 64, 89
Spalding, Capt., 53

Spencer-Pierce House, 1, 9
- Garrison House, 9
Spencer-Pierce-Little Farm, 1, 4, 14fn
Spencer-Pierce-Little House, 2
Spring, Captains
- father and son, 53
Stanley, Capt., 53
Stanley, Mrs., 51
steam wagon, 13
Stedman house, 53
Stickney, T. B.
- cashier, First National Bank, 28
Stone, Capt., 53
Stone, Eben F., Col., 36, 74
- Civil War, 48th MA Regiment, 36, 74
- Congress, 3 terms, 36, 74
- president, City Council, 36
- lawyer, 36, 74
- MA Legislature, 36
- mayor, 36, 74
Stone, Harlan Fiske, Judge
- school reunion, 14
Stone, Jacob, bank cashier
- First National Bank, 38
- Ocean National Bank, 38

streets
- Allen Street, 46
- Boardman Street, 45
- Bromfield Street, 21, 44, 52, 77
- Carter Street, 39
- Chestnut Street, 21
- Devon Road, 57
- Essex Street, 29, 36, 39
- Federal Street, 31, 46, 53, 77
- Green Street, 13, 50
- Greenleaf Street, 36, 74
- Hale's Court, 31, 78
- Harris Street, 13

High Street, 15, 36, 39, 44, 46, 49, 50, 51, 52, 52fn 58, 87, 88
Inn Street, 3, 31, 78
Lime Street, 53
Market Square, 18, 27, 78, 79
Market Street, 38, 87fn, 90
Marlboro Street, 20, 21
Merrimac Street, 31, 78, 79
Milk Street, 46
Monroe Street, 77
Munroe Street, 31
North Street, 77
Oakland Street, 77
Olive Street, 50
Orange Street, 46
Parsons Street, 50
Pleasant Street, 3, 29, 31, 63, 78
Prince Place, 31, 34, 78
Purchase Street, 46
Salem Street, 31, 77
South Street, 77
State Street, 10, 27, 28, 28fn, 29, 30, 31, 34, 36, 44, 74, 78, 90
Threadneedle Alley, 90
Three Roads, 87
Tracy Place, 31
Washington Street, 13, 38, 45
Water Street, 18fn, 19, 21, 24, 33, 77, 78, 79
sugar, 11, 21, 24, 25, 46
Sumner, Eben
    director, First National Bank, 28
Sumner, Swasey and Currier, 18, 35, 37, 75, 78
Swasey and Sherrill
    shoe manufacturer, 3
Swasey, William H., Mr., 35, 36

amateur artist, 35, 36
E. P. Dodge Mfg. Co., 3
Sumner, Swasey and Currier, 35
treasurer, Towle Mfg. Co., 35
Swift and Co., 18, 78
Symonds, Capt., 53

T

telegraph, 85
telephone, 12, 29, 41, 57, 85
telescope, 51
tenants, 11, 14fn
Thurlow, Paul, Capt., 53
Thurston, William
    director, First National Bank, 28
Titcomb, Albert C., 42
    Civil War, 42
    mayor, 42
    treasurer, Lamson Store Service Co., 42
Titcomb, Paul, 45
Toppan, Charles, 40
Toppan, Robert, 40
torch-light parade, 10
Towle Company, 32
Towle Manufacturing Co., 35
Tracy house, 50
trade
    Calcutta, 18, 78
    China, 78
Trask, Mr., 53
trolley cars manufacturing, 32
Troy, New York, 41, 90
Turkey Hill, 77
typhoon, 52
    Indian Ocean, 45, 47

V

Varina, Capt., 53
Vermont, 42

vessels, 5fn, 17, 18, 22, 64, 74, 78, 79
Victor Manufacturing Co., 46
voting, 57

W

Welch, Richard, 46
West Indies, 13, 24, 25, 52, 75
West Indies trade, 21
Western railroads, 42
whale-oil lamps, 11
wharf, 18, 51, 79
    Bayley's Wharf, 23, 24, 25
    Central Wharf, 18
    City Wharf, 18, 79
    Ferry Wharf, 50
wharves, 11, 17, 18, 21, 74, 75, 78
Wheelwright Fund, 51, 80
Wheelwright, William, 80
William, Capt., 47
Wills, Capt., 53
Wills, Henry, Mrs., 12
Withington, Leonard, Rev., 38
Withington, Nathan Noyes, 38
    Civil War, 11th MA Infantry, 38
    editor, *Newburyport Herald*, 38
    Veteran Reserve Corps, 38
Witteveld, Chris
    friend of Waldo Peirce, 90fn, 91
Woods, Capt., 53

Y

Yerxa and Co., 18, 79
Yerxa's groceries, 19

Z

ZR-2 airship, 62

ABOUT THE AUTHOR

Margaret "Marge" Peckham Motes has been doing research for over thirty years in partnership with her husband, Jesse "Skip" Hogan Motes, on historical research, their family genealogies, writing, and publishing – Marge, the researcher, Skip the writer and lecturer. He has given many talks in the Newburyport area on their collaborative work.

Marge was a volunteer at the Museum of Old Newbury (previously, Historical Society of Old Newbury) answering queries from across the country for the society for fourteen years and on special projects during that time period.

She enjoys finding historical articles buried in early newspapers and compiling them into monographs.

Marge and Skip moved to Newburyport in 1995 – both have New England roots – and have delved deeply into Newburyport's history. They currently are working on several new books on Newburyport.

The Motes are prize-winning authors and researchers. The National Genealogical Society awarded them the 1995 prize for Sources and Methods for their book on a South Carolina colonial settlement. The Newburyport Preservation Trust selected them for their 2017 Award for Excellence in Historical Research and Writing. In 2018, the Mayor of Newburyport awarded them a Distinguished Service Award for their promotion of art and history in the City of Newburyport. The award included accommodations from the Massachusetts Senate and House of Representatives.

Skip and Marge Motes.
Photograph by Kathleen Downey – Nov. 2013.

www.ingramcontent.com/pod-product-compliance
Ingram Content Group UK Ltd.
Pitfield, Milton Keynes, MK11 3LW, UK
UKHW021309180426
11947UKWH00015B/1121